i

Digitally Famous:
for Entrepreneurs

Digitally Famous:
for
Entrepreneurs

Brandy Nagel

Second Edition, MAY 2017

Copyright © 2017 by Brandy Nagel

All rights reserved. Published in the United States.

http://digitallyfamousthebook.com

Graphics used with permission from Microsoft.

Printed in the United States of America

10 9 8 7 6 5 4 3 2

Copyright © 2017 Brandy Stanfield-Nagel

ISBN-13: 978-1477471326

DEDICATION

To my dear friends and colleagues at

Georgia Tech and Grupo Guayacán.

CONTENTS

ACKNOWLEDGMENTS

Anita Hampl

Jenny Munn

Joey Sargent

Introduction

Included here are practical ideas on how to improve your online and off-line visibility in your industry, community, and neighborhood. The following tips and social media tools will help you make a name for yourself on the web and in person.

These skills will you serve you well in other areas of life, too – being elected, getting promoted or just becoming slightly famous.

Parts of this book are based on my experiences as a reluctant entrepreneur. I was laid-off in January 2009 and landed my first client the next day. Owning my own business was an appealing idea. As I worked to "get my name out there," I met wonderful people. And received offers and opportunities that fit with my personal and professional goals. The best part was when I was recognized in a coffee shop. I had made a name for myself in my community. I went home and called my mom: "Mom, I'm getting slightly famous!"

To this day, I attend events relevant to my career, meet with people in my industry, and regularly share a cup of coffee with small business owners.

This book is tactical in nature – not a lot of theory. In here, you will find the practical details of how to design business cards, when to connect with potential clients via LinkedIn® and why you should volunteer.

Note the icons that will help you along the way:

 Here's a bright idea

 An assignment or exercise for you to try

 A question for you to consider

 Search for this on Google®

 Valuable information

Screenshots are included throughout the book in an effort to make the connection for visual learners. A list of links is included in the back for easy reference.

I hope the techniques in this book work for you as you grow your business and look for your next big adventure.

Brandy Nagel

1 Branding

Everyone has a brand, whether they want one or not. It is the collection of interactions and experiences with you – positive, negative, and neutral. It is your reputation.

Your personal brand as a business owner is tied to the reputation of your business. So, let's talk about personal brand for a moment.

You can't control what people think about you. **However**, you can *influence* what they hear, see, and read. When you Google® your name, what results do you get?

_____

_____

_____

Now Google® your name and then click on *images* to see how you look online. The visual elements are a big part of perception.

What is the visual foundation of your brand? Do your Google images reflect the brand you want to project?

_____

_____

_____

The picture you select to represent yourself is crucial. More on this in Chapter 6. And how you dress to impress the world every day matters, too.

What can you do or wear that will enhance your brand? Madeleine Albright had her pins (Read My Pins: Stories from a Diplomat's Jewel Box by Madeleine Albright, available on Amazon.com.) Perhaps you are known for a particular style of dress – preppy, professional, vintage, or avant-garde. Perhaps, like Ms. Albright, you wear accessories that set you apart: snappy ties, cool purses, the latest gadgets, funky spectacles. Whatever it is that makes you stand out, do yourself a favor and make it something that comes naturally and feels comfortable. You will be more consistent if the style suits you – and more likely to break from your brand if it feels awkward to tiresome.

Do you have a "trademark saying" that people recognize? Or perhaps you have a charming accent? I have an acquaintance who always wears the same wonderful perfume – I can identify her by fragrance!

I have two important elements of my personal brand: cool eyeglasses, and curly red hair. Other, smaller elements are part of my brand, too, like using black ink pens, (rather than blue) and flat shoes (you'll never see me wobbling around in heels.) These small details add up to make an impression.

A strong personal brand is built by making consistent choices – in how we do business, in how we act and dress. How do you want to be perceived? Books have been written about authenticity and the bottom line is: **it is best to just be you**.

What details (large or small) can you commit to being part of your brand?

_____

_____

_____

Taking it Online

 Take a moment to review your Online ID Calculator at www.onlineidcalculator.com. This will tell you if you are digitally distinct, or digitally disastrous, based on the volume and relevance of your Google results and other online indicators.

(Extra credit homework: check out your profile on pipl.com and spokeo.com. See how much information you can find about yourself.)

What if you have a name similar to a celebrity? If you share your name with a famous actor, politician, or criminal, for example, it might be helpful to use a middle initial, (Brad L. Pitt) or a variation on your name (Donald Draper.)

Consider the plight of the person with a common name – Tom Smith, for example. Tom needs to distinguish himself with a tagline, title, or strong branding.

Creating a tagline and title

Creating a title or tagline (and adding it to your business cards) can make you more memorable and can help people help you land your next client.

Select a title that has implications to create interest. You can call yourself a "sales executive" - but so can a million other people. Try "Quota Buster" or "Deal Maker."

Jim Stroud is a *Searchologist*, a person adept at online research.

Other interesting titles:

- Evangelist
- Rainmaker
- Chief Marketing Ninja
  Exercise: Google® "cool job titles"

_____

_____

_____

You can make up a title for yourself, as I did:

Brandy Nagel, Marketing Catalyst

If you make up a title, people will ask you to explain it. Be prepared.

Q: "Marketing Catalyst? So what does that mean exactly?"

A: "It means that I make marketing happen."

Now, I'm all in favor of creativity here, but not at the expense of clarity. If you replace windshields for a living, your card should not say "Vision Clearance Engineer." (Hat tip to Dudley Dawson, author of _Life in The Cubicle_ for that little gem.) Skip the gobbledygook. Say it as simply as possible.

Exercise: Google®: "gobbledygook manifesto"

Remember this essential principle of branding:
Be consistent. Although healthy brands (and healthy people) evolve over time, core values remain stable.
Many celebrities have a **brand sheet** for use when they are considering sponsorships, brand extensions, joint ventures, or endorsements. For a peek into how the famous people do it, look at this list of brand values from soccer player Michael Owen:

- Fit & Healthy
- First Class
- Successful
- Clean & Fresh
- Global
- Stylish
- Charismatic
- Articulate
- Dynamic
- Enthusiastic
- Instinctive
- Respected

What characteristics do you want to have associated with your brand?

_____

_____

_____

What can be done about a bad reputation? Glad you asked. A
bad reputation (deserved or not) can put a damper on business.
First thing is to try to correct whatever the perceived problem
is. (I figure you've already tried that, though.) Second step is to
fill the internet with positives so the negative becomes a
smaller portion of content about you. This might mean
commenting on blogs, creating a YouTube channel, writing
LinkedIn recommendations, and so on. You'll read more about
all of these in later chapters.

Take a moment to jot down notes on your brand here:

_____

_____

_____

_____

2 Cards, E-mail & Voicemail

One item you should never be without: **business cards.**

Fortunately, online resources make it easy and affordable.

VistaPrint offers 250 cards for under $20. (You might select some options – like metallic accents – that push the price up a bit.)

Typical business cards have a company logo, a title, and contact info.

So, let's start with the easy stuff. You will be handing your card to people you've just met, people you want to stay in touch with. Commonly, we expect people to contact us via phone or e-mail. Do you need to include a mailing address? Only if you have a retail location or office. If you work from home, avoid giving out your address, use a P.O. Box or just the name of the city.

Of these three, your name is the most critical item to get right. It sounds obvious, but think carefully about how you want to present yourself. The name you use on your cards should match your LinkedIn® profile, online presence, networking profile and any other items you create for your visibility campaign.

Exercise: search for your name on LinkedIn®. How many people have a similar name?

Can you distinguish yourself with a small change? Perhaps a middle initial, a nickname in quotations, or your maiden name?

_____

_____

_____

 If your name is unique and locals have a hard time saying it, add a pronunciation tip to your card.

Designing your card

Rules for the first time you order cards:

1. Use a light background with dark lettering, with high contrast.
2. The font should be between 7.5 point and 10 point.
3. Avoid childish or cartoon-y clip art. (More on this later.)
4. Order 250 cards the first time you place an order.
5. Use a highly legible font - not a fancy italic script.
6. Check and double-check the phone number and spelling.
7. When in doubt, keep it simple. Less is more.

> Art
> Vandelay
> **Vandelay Industries**
> *Import/Export*
> *Latex Goods*
>
> NYC, NY
> 212-555-1234

The *next* time you order cards you can experiment with color, font, design, and content.

I recently had a woman fuss at me for the "wasted space" on my card. "You could add a value statement here," she pointed out, referring to the blank backside of my business card.

Your card is the single most important piece of personal branding you will ever create. It is likely the only item that people will ever completely read and keep. Your card must reflect you. I am happy with the design of my card and I continue to tweak and improve it over time.

Design tip: consider designing your card to be horizontal instead of vertical - eye-catching.

Use other printed materials as inspiration. Compare the look and feel of these catalogs: Tiffany's, Pottery Barn, and Lillian Vernon. Which one is your card most like?

Glossy cards look more expensive, but glossy paper shows fingerprints as ugly smudges. Matte paper is also easier to write on if you want to add a note to your card.

One way to select a unique design on VistaPrint is to sort cards by popularity – and then look at the least popular. Some of these are unpopular because they are unattractive – but honestly, I think some of the most popular card designs are hideous. You may find a hidden jewel among the least popular designs – a design that will be unique and professional.

Tip: visit www.vistaprint.com and ask for product samples.

Creative folks should include a link to their online portfolio. (More on online portfolios later)

Multi-lingual? Add something like this: "Fluent in Spanish, conversant in French."

What critical pieces of information should you include on your card?

Say cheese!

Should you include a photo of yourself on your card?

It's common in some areas - real estate agents often have a head shot on their card. If you are presenting yourself as a consultant, and you are photogenic, you could add a picture. Make it a photo that represents you well.

But, generally speaking, those cards are more expensive, and unless your career path is based on your appearance - say acting, broadcasting, or public speaking - I think it's not worth the extra bucks.

Spotted: I just received a business card that included:

We met at _____.

She wrote the date and name of the event as we exchanged cards. Brilliant idea! If you are attending a week-long conference, and anticipate meeting 250 people, have a set of cards printed just for the occasion. Add "We met at the 2017 Poultry Expo, Atlanta GA" below your name, but above your contact points.

What to leave off your card:

- Fax number - unless it is crucial to your business
- Irrelevant images or graphics, such as a quill, fountain pen, slide ruler. (Clip art must die! More on this later.)
- Images of the globe – unless you are multi-lingual.
- Giant eyes – unless you are an eye care professional.

No need to include the word "e-mail" in front of your e-mail. We all recognize the format of an e-mail address, so the descriptor is not needed. The same goes for "telephone," and other points of contact. Try the one letter designation:

> H: for Home phone
> O: for Office phone
> C: for Cell phone

DIY Cards

Making your own cards at home has certain advantages. You can customize cards for particular events. You can create truly unique cards. However, printing your own cards can be time consuming and more expensive than ordering from an online printer. If you are determined to print your own, keep these tips in mind:

First, clip art can be great – or it can be awful. The days of cartoonish illustration are over. The trend is icons and photos. That is, high quality, legal, royalty-free images. You can find them by searching the web using these key phrases: creative commons, free.

Here are a few sources I found for photos and images:

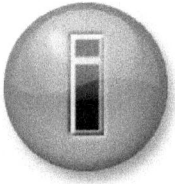

- EveryStockPhoto.com – Indexes over a million Creative Commons (CC) photos for your use.

- Wikimedia Commons – The clearing area for the Wikimedia projects' CC files.

- Flickr Creative Commons search – Search Flickr for derivatives of the CC licensing.

Remember, an *icon* is a stylized illustration that expresses just one idea, *clip art* is an illustration of a person, place, or thing. Icons are more powerful than clip art because they leave no room for interpretation. Clip art comes is many styles and is often vague. This is why clip art must die.

An icon:

Clip art:

Second, perforated cards are so last century. Use Avery Clean Edge Business cards, or something similar. Avery offers free downloadable software to help you design and print a decent business card.

Finally, you must take an oath. Raise your right hand and repeat after me:

I solemnly swear to not use perforated cards, so help me.

X _____

Standing out from the crowd

A few cards I've collected over the years stand out:

- An art director with a scalloped edge to her card - elegant and tactile.
- A marketing pro with his info on the back of a collectible holographic card.

What can you do to make your card unique?

Quick Response Codes

Recently, I've seen more and more business cards with QR codes. My personal favorite was from Erik Wolf of Zero-G Creative. Scanning his QR code with my smart phone took me to a unique webpage that said: "We've met, haven't we? Thanks for keeping in touch!"

QR codes have great potential. However, a QR code that goes to your regular website is a lost opportunity. Direct the person to something unique: a special webpage, an online portfolio, or a special **about.me** page. Plan to maintain that page for the long term.

Moo cards

Moo cards are a unique and fun option. They come in a variety of sizes including non-standard sizes. The cards are a great choice for artists as they are an easy way to show off your artwork. At $20 for 50 cards, moo cards are more expensive than other options. But sometimes you need a dazzling card to win an opportunity.

Always carry cards with you – in a business card case that will protect them. My favorite is Filexec MiniCase (frosted or translucent), available on Amazon.

> QR codes should be at least one inch square for best printing results, and best scanning results.

Location, location, location!

If you conduct business in multiple locations, consider ordering two sets of cards (one for each location, with a local phone number on each) or indicate the dual nature of your business on your cards. Check out Morty's card for inspiration.

Morty Seinfeld
Raincoat Salesman

Inventor of the beltless trench coat

New York City/Del Boca Vista, FL

Ring! Ring!

When a caller dials your phone number, what do they hear? Will you be the one to answer that phone number 100% of the time? Or is there a chance that your kooky Aunt Zelda will pick up and forget to give you the message?

It is important to have a local phone number.

Here's why: From the point of view of a potential client, if a person says they live nearby, but the area code is not local, it creates *uncertainty*. And that's bad. Get a local phone number for where you want to do business.

You may want to set up a unique phone number for your business. Consider Google's free Voice service. From the *Google Voice* website:

Google Voice enhances the existing capabilities of your phone, regardless of which phone or carrier you have - for free. It also gives you:

- *One number - Use a single number that rings you anywhere.*
- *Online voicemail - Get transcribed messages delivered to your inbox.*

 **Greetings!**

Your recorded message (or greeting) should be simple and professional. If you can't get it to sound the way you want, ask someone with a good voice and pleasant accent to help you.

Exercise: Call yourself right now and listen to your own message.

_____

_____

_____

If it is time to re-record your message, try this: *Hello, you have reached [your name here]. I am away from the phone at the moment, please leave a message and I will return your call.*

Or: *You've reached [your name here]. He is away from the phone at the moment.*

(This is a good idea if you are a man, and you ask a lady to record the greeting for you.)

If you have a name that works for a man or a woman (Jerry/Gerrie) consider this:

You've reached [your name here]. She is away from the phone at the moment...

Tip: Record the greeting in a quiet place with no background noise. Call the number to hear how it sounds. Re-record as needed to eliminate distracting sounds, long pauses or a less than smooth delivery.

Tips for having a great recording voice:

- Drink plenty of water before making the recording.
- Avoid dairy products for a few hours before recording.
- Some people swear by gargling with salt water, but it tastes terrible.

Having a phone number for your campaign is a good idea; having a unique e-mail is a **great** idea.

E-mails from older domains (aol.com, for example) are thought by some techies to be a sign of a non-tech savvy person. Not a problem in some professions - a kiss of death in others.

Ah, a blank slate - now you can create an e-mail handle that represents the real you!

Not so fast. The name you use for your new e-mail address must be professional. You may be a "foxy grandpa," but your future clients and business associates do not need to know that right now.

It is likely that tom.smith@gmail.com is no longer available on Gmail, so play around with your name and initials until you hit on something that works. Use periods (or dots) for emphasis. You can use capital letters when you print the e-mail address on your business cards. Avoid using your birth year as numbers - no need to reveal your age.

Tom.smith.CPA

Thomas.smith.accountant

BeancounterTomSmith

Along with your new e-mail handle, it is time to create a new signature block.

Your sig block is part of your branding, so give it some thought. Here are a few tips:

- A long signature block undermines your authority and makes you look like a poser.
- Basic contact points are all we need.
- Keep it in standard colors, (probably black or blue) and a TrueType font

My favorite sig block looks something like this:

Name | email | phone number | c: cell phone
Web address

Note: That vertical line between the data points is called a *pipe* and it can be found in the special symbols section of your favorite word processing program. Your best bet is to design the sig block in Word, then copy and paste it into your e-mail settings.

- Avoid using any clip art, graphics, or animation.
- Use a standard font, the same size as the rest of your email.
- Keep it simple.

Include your web address or your LinkedIn® URL (personalize your URL before adding – instructions on this later.) Creative types should have an about.me page, or a link to an online portfolio.

You may wish to put an inspiring quote or a witticism in your signature block. I love this habit –just remember to change it every year or so.

3 Networking

Networking is How People Get Clients

Just like the "good old days," it is who you know – and how well you connect with them. When selling to big business, you always want to by-pass gatekeepers by having a connection inside. Using this "back door method" is more likely to get your business card into the right hands. It is the difference between a warm introduction and a cold call.

> The purpose of a networking profile is to show it to people to get you closer to discovering opportunities...to provide a spark to help them point you to other people who may point you to opportunities.
> – Lance Weatherby, technology entrepreneur

Networking Profile – Also Known as a Marketing Plan

During a visibility campaign, you should plan to have coffee with bunches of people. Coffee (or tea) is a great way to meet people and connect with opportunities. To make the best use of your time – and the other person's time – a networking profile can make a meeting more productive.

A résumé tells the reader your work history; your networking profile helps people understand your ambitions for the future. A networking profile is always one page (front and back.) If you can't fit it on one page, you are doing it wrong.

 **Tip**: Check out the fill in the blank format in the back of the book.

At the top of the page are your contact points.

Name

Phone and e-mail address

Next comes a summary – just two or three sentences about your skills, who you are, what you're capable of.

Be accurate. Be concise. Be bold.

You'll never get what you want if you don't ask for it. Identify your goal right here as a Profile Statement.

- Consulting work
- Contract or freelance work
- Public speaking opportunities

Include the high points, the relevant parts. Leave off the stuff that is irrelevant, or that you never want to do again.

Use the most concise descriptors possible: rather than former Marine, say veteran.

A few other examples:

- Masters of business becomes MBA

- Marketing professional becomes Marketer

Play with the order of your words to save space.

Graduated from Wharton's graduate business school becomes Wharton MBA

Next, include your credentials or education.

- Microsoft certified

- Licensed esthetician

Brainstorm with friends, family, and colleagues to create a list of skills and areas of expertise. What makes your business unique? Is it a particular combination of offerings or skills?

Finally, include a list of companies you'd like to work for, or a profile of your target companies. This target list will help people to make the meaningful connections you need.

Now, **print this document** and carry it with you in a portfolio or folder whenever you leave the house. When anyone (and I mean anyone) asks, "what do you do for a living?" you can respond by saying, "Here's a summary of my business and who is a good referral for me...." Give a moment to skim the document and then point out the target companies at the bottom. Ask, "Do you have contacts at any of these companies? I'd love to make a connection and see if they need my services."

Ideally, the document is a "take away" – meaning the person takes it home and reviews it more thoroughly. I don't need to tell you, but I will anyway, this document needs to be 100% correct including spelling, grammar, and punctuation.

Now that you've made the connection and provided a networking profile, what is the goal? To **schedule a meeting** with a person who works at your target company. Ideally, this would be in person, but a phone conversation can be effective also.

So now, it is time to craft a good "tell me about yourself" (TMAY) also known as an elevator pitch. Try these starters:

My background includes ….
I studied….
Unlike most people, I've been fortunate to…
Most recently, I've specialized in…
For my next opportunity, I'm looking for…
While at Kramerica, I worked with…

What key points will you mention in your pitch?

_____
_____
_____
_____
_____
_____
_____
_____

4 Get Off the Couch

Get off the couch.

I don't know how to say it any simpler. The couch is not your friend. Sitting at home, watching reruns will not get you where you want to go.

"But I'm so tired!" you say in a whiny voice.

"Going out is so expensive," you protest.

Or maybe your objection is traffic or family responsibilities or lack of time.

Yeah, yeah, yeah. I'm calling baloney on all that.

Exercise: Google® Gary Vaynerchuk "do what you love"

You have a choice. You can veg out on the couch or get up and do something. Sometimes it is exhausting. Sometimes it ends up not being worth your time. Nevertheless, you can almost always find something to do that is a better option than sitting on the couch.

Homework: Scout Plancast.com and EventBrite.com for activities in your area.

Meetups

Meetups are a wonderful phenomenon. Before Meetup.com, people sat at home in the dark. And before indoor living was invented, people sat around in caves. Meetups are a modern miracle.

In my modest town of 80,000, we have approximately 420 groups that meet weekly or monthly. Seriously.

And look at the astounding variety: Stepmoms, Sisters in Christ, Female Kickball, Horror Movie Fans, Real Estate Investing, Native American Flute Circle, Psychic Adventures, Let's Converse in Spanish, Goorin Brothers Hat Lovers, Mah-Jong Madness, Atlanta Pirates and Wenches Guild, Motorcycle Club and so much more.

Conclusion: Whether you are a Goth or a Granny, there is something here for you to participate in, join, or attend.

Exercise: Visit www.meetup.com right now. Enter your ZIP code and find a group nearby.

_____

_____

_____

_____

Toastmasters

Toastmasters must be one of the most interesting groups in the United States – errr, in the world. Incredibly affordable, exceptionally effective, if you are interested in improving your speaking skills, this group can help you learn.

From their website, www.toastmasters.org

Toastmasters International is a world leader in communication and leadership development. Today, our membership is 270,000 strong. These members improve their speaking and leadership skills by attending one of the 13,000 clubs that make up our global network of meeting locations.

Membership in Toastmasters is one of the greatest investments you can make in yourself. At $36 every six months, it is also one of the most cost-effective skill-building tools available anywhere.

How Does It Work? A Toastmasters meeting is a learn-by-doing workshop in which participants hone their speaking and leadership skills in a no-pressure atmosphere. A typical group has 20 to 40 members who meet weekly, biweekly or monthly. A typical meeting lasts 60–90 minutes.

Toastmasters is a non-profit organization developing public speaking and leadership skills through practice and feedback in local clubs since 1924.

$36 for six months is an incredible bargain, and the Toastmaster method of learn by doing has been working for a long time. My experience with Toastmasters groups is that they attract friendly, optimistic people who welcome new people to the group.

Volunteering

Volunteering feels good. Giving your time and talent can empower you. Helping to make something happen or to improve a situation builds self-esteem, and connects you to

29

your community. Furthermore, it puts you in touch with a new circle of people.

Two great resources for volunteering: www.volunteermatch.org and www.micromentor.org.

Consider volunteering with a local professional association – or volunteer at a big conference. Or start something new.

In 2009, Jason Brett was looking for a new job and he hit on the idea of putting together an unconference for his industry, product management and marketing. With a few helping hands, and lots of encouragement, Jason secured a venue, sponsors, and more than 200 participants.

An *unconference* is similar to a conference,

> Everybody can be great... because anybody can serve. You don't have to have a college degree to serve. You don't have to make your subject and verb agree to serve.
> - Martin Luther King, Jr.

but the agenda is set by the people who attend, at the beginning of the event. ProductCamp Atlanta is in its third year and is still going strong. And Jason? He landed a great job with a great company about 30 days after his wildly successful unconference.

Now What?

When you start networking, or meeting up or volunteering, you may find that you have a bunch of items to add to your "to do" list. That's great! Hop to it! But what will you stop doing? (Beside no longer watching re-runs of LOST.)

There are only 24 hours in a day. You have to spend ever so many hours on sleeping, eating, and general life maintenance.

So what will you eliminate that will free up time for this new endeavor?

Will you outsource some chores? Say no to meaningless social obligations? Maybe you need to simplify your life with an easier grooming routine or easy care clothes. What will you stop doing?

Stop Doing list

_____

_____

_____

5 Become a Verb

Become a verb.

Better yet, become a transitive verb.

When I worked a corporate gig, the head of the legal department was Kristen McGuffey. When I had a legal document (a contract or a lease agreement, for example) I took it to

> A transitive verb has two characteristics. First, it is an action verb, expressing a doable activity like kick, want, paint, write, eat, clean, etc. Second, it must have a direct object, something or someone who receives the action of the verb.
>
> - Robin L. Simmons

Kristen and she reviewed and approved – or revised or rejected – the document. I would "McGuffey" the documents – that is, take them through the process of legal review.

Thus, this definition:

Mc·Guf'fey (mak·guf'i), v.t. & i.

1. To present for inspection an item, specifically, any document or policy, seeking formal approval for accuracy and suitability, as, *Please **McGuffey** this contract before we sign it.* **2.** To identify errors or flaws, esp. in documents or policies, (see LITIGATION AVOIDANCE) prior to publication, as, *"Thank God, we **McGuffied** this brochure before we went to print!"*

It's shorthand, no doubt. But, it became easier to say, "I'll McGuffey it" to my boss than to say, "I'll take this to Legal for review." Plus, it sounds cooler. And cool points are crucial.

So, what is it that you do? (Choose an action verb)

Advise	Empower	Investigate	Rally
Analyze	Encourage	Invigorate	Recruit
Assist			Rescue
Awaken	Energize	Jolt	Serve
Conquer	Engage	Lead	Study
Convert	Find	Organize	Support
Counsel	Fortify	Pamper	Survey
Delight	Guide	Persuade	Tame
Educate	Help	Prepare	Teach
Elevate	Inspire	Protect	Verify
Eliminate	Instruct	Pursue	Woo
			Worship

From Peter's Playable Actions

And who or what do you do it to? (Choose a direct object)

- People: Kids, students, elders, athletes, artists, entrepreneurs, programmers, volunteers, soccer moms, business owners, rabbis, travelers, CEOs
- Ideas: initiatives, plans, concepts, campaigns
- Things: databases, piles of paper, houses, corporations
- Places: classrooms, prisons, offices, worship houses, gardens

_____

_____

_____

What problem do you solve?

Examples:

I'm a professional organizer; I help people organize their home and work space.

I'm a landscape architect; I make your yard look fabulous.

Are you a Paper Tamer or a Horse Whisperer?

_____

_____

_____

It was always my dream to become a verb.

- Judd Apatow, producer

6 You -- Online

Social media is a way to...

- inspire
- entertain
- educate
- inform
- recruit
- persuade
- listen
- learn
- share
- connect

Using...

- written words
- audio (music and spoken word)
- visual (photos, graphics, and movies)
- interactive (maps and games)

Presenting Your Accomplishments Online

There are many ways to promote yourself and your accomplishments online.

www.clippings.me is a great tool for writers – and people who aren't writers, but want to show case their writing skills.

www.visualcv.com is, as the name suggests, a site for creating a visually rich résumé

Online Visuals

A photo of your poodle Frank with bunny ears attached to his head is not a good substitute for a decent headshot. Some folks have one picture and use it consistently on all forms of media – business card, LinkedIn® profile, etc. Others change their profile picture regularly to keep it fresh.

Have you put off posting a photo because you are concerned about appearing too old? Well, I made up a rule about that. (More about making up rules later.)

Rule: The age of your profile photo should not be older than 10% of your age.

Thus, a 43-year-old person can use a picture from four years ago, and my uncle Fred can use a picture from his early 90s because he is 103 years old.

A profile picture can be black and white or a colorful Warhol-inspired design. There are many options, but essentially, the picture needs to look like you. Try to crop the picture so you are the focus – crop out distracting backgrounds and make sure there is not too much space above your head (makes you look short). Adjust the color – focus on getting the color of your skin accurate – the color of your clothing is secondary. You may also want to try http://makeup.pho.to/.

Alternatives for the camera shy:

- Use a baby picture (your own baby picture, not just a random baby picture) or a picture of you as a youngster. This is great for Facebook®, but not LinkedIn.

- Crop your photo to highlight just one feature of your face– the feature you like best about yourself (your eyes, or a smile and a dimple.) Check out Charity's profile below.
- Create a cartoon avatar or a manga. http://faceyourmanga.com/
- Make a logo, like my friend Dave Graham. Dave is a graphic design instructor – so a logo suits him particularly well.

Charity Newsome
Experienced Professional in Marketing and Communications
Greater Atlanta Area | Marketing and Advertising

You can do something silly like use Marilyn Monroe's photo as your own – or George Clooney or whoever else blows your skirts. Ultimately, if your intention is to be recognized in your community (virtual or real), a faux photo won't get you to your goal.

Once you've decided on your visual representation, visit www.gravatar.com and create your globally recognized avatar. This will provide a consistent image of you on blogs comments and other locations online.

Online Reputation Management

"Search engines and social media sites now play a central role in building one's identity online," says Mary Madden, Senior Research Specialist of the Pew Internet & American Life Project. "Many users are learning and refining their approach as they go – changing privacy settings on profiles, customizing who can see certain updates and deleting unwanted information about them that appears online."

Do you Google® yourself? That is, do you put your name into Google® or another major search engine and review the results?

Exercise: Go Google® yourself. (Go ahead, I'll wait right here.)

_____

_____

My Aunt Gerri came to town recently visiting from out west. We had not seen each other in several years. At dinner she surprised me with "Hey, I googled you – looks like you're doing all kinds of neat stuff." My Aunt Gerri uses Google® – and so do the majority of your prospects and potential clients.

Rather than trying to remember to Google® yourself on a regular schedule, set up a **Google alert** for your name. If you have a common name, you may need to add another word or phrase to receive more accurate results. So, for example, Tom Smith, a CPA, might set up a Google alert like this: **"Tom Smith" CPA Chicago**

 **Bonus tip:** set up a Google alert for all of the important people in your life, and for the companies you want to work with so you receive the latest news. Visit http://www.google.com/alerts and follow the instructions.

So now, you will be notified when your name pops up on Google's radar. If you find a result that does not represent you the way you want, you can contact that website and ask to have your name removed.

What else can you do to get your name out onto the World Wide Web?

_____

_____

_____

The four most important social web sites are Facebook®, Twitter®, LinkedIn®, and You Tube. Let's discuss them next.

http://namechk.com/

Check to see if your desired *username* or *vanity url* is still available at dozens of popular social websites. Prevent confusion by consistently using one name.

7 LinkedIn® 101

LinkedIn® helps me make meaningful connections with clients, former co-workers, and business associates. And I use it to keep track of friends. LinkedIn® helped me land my last two jobs and a good bit of freelance work.

<u>How much time is this going to take?</u>

Depends. I spend **about 15 minutes twice a week** - helping others and following up on connections, introductions and relationships.

It may seem like a big-time investment – particularly if your current responsibilities are demanding, but the time invested in developing and maintaining my network has always been a good investment for me.

What Exactly is LinkedIn®?

LinkedIn® is Facebook® for business people. What sets it apart from Facebook® and Twitter® is the understanding that people join LinkedIn® with the goal of

Linked in.

expanding their business or developing their career. In other words, it's acceptable to show your business card. Much like real world network meetings, professionals interact on LinkedIn® with the intention of making business connections.

Why LinkedIn® is Important

If the possibility of easing by gatekeepers to talk directly with decision-makers sounds appealing, then LinkedIn® is the place for you. LinkedIn® provides a platform for you to research individuals who you know will directly add value to your endeavors.

Imagine walking into a business function where potential clients are introduced to you, colleagues acknowledge your accomplishments without your prompting, and you're in the spotlight for sharing answers for inquiries related to your industry. LinkedIn® makes these scenarios a daily reality.

LinkedIn' s tools help you to identify, research, follow-up, engage and maintain your contacts in one place. This tool set is unmatched by other social networks.

Before Creating a Profile

Setting up a LinkedIn® account is a quick and easy process. You literally could set up an account in five minutes, upload your résumé, and be set for life. However, speed is not the main objective. Rushing could lead to a sloppy profile that doesn't represent you well. Let's talk through the major sections and identify the important parts.

Essentially your profile stands as a résumé, business card, and elevator speech all rolled into one. Before posting any information, there are some proactive steps you can take to ensure your profile works for you and not against you.

First, think about exactly who will be looking for you on LinkedIn®.

Your profile should:

* contain lots of keywords that he or she will use to

search you out.

- highlight your education, expertise, and accomplishments.
- serve as a platform for thought leadership.

With that said, keep in mind that in the business world, you have direct competition and it's no different on LinkedIn®. Thoroughly researching competitor profiles is a simple step all savvy professionals can take before creating (or updating) a profile. If you want to become the go-to professional for your industry, it's best to analyze who's holding the top spots.

How do you find the profiles of people to model?

A general rule of thumb is that a high search engine ranking stands as a good indicator of a professional who's doing well on LinkedIn® for a particular niche. Use Google® search as a fast way to retrieve all the profiles for a keyword on LinkedIn®.

1. Go to Google.com.
2. Type in the search string site:linkedin.com "your keywords."
3. Replace the phrase "your keywords" with terms related to your specialty.

Focus on the top ten search results. Your goal is for your profile to be listed in the top three results for your keywords.

Like other social media sites, LinkedIn® members commonly

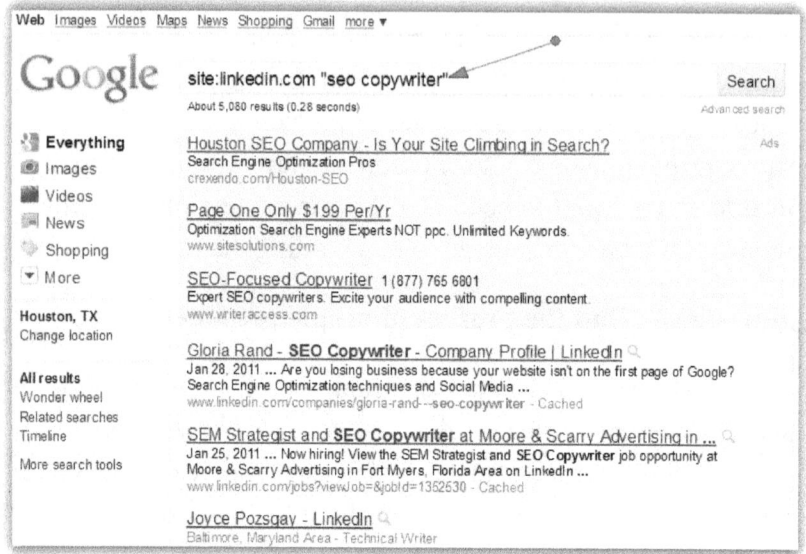

use the search feature within the site to locate people they're seeking. A high-ranking profile ensures you're being seen by recruiters and hiring managers.

Visit each of the top listed profiles and take note of how they're representing themselves for your market. In particular, pay attention to the keywords used and the headlines.

How to Set-up a Basic Account

The basic membership to LinkedIn® is free, and is the best choice for the majority of users. As a business owner, you may wish to buy a premium membership for a month or two to use the enhanced features and pump up your pipeline.

To get started, go to LinkedIn.com and select "Join Today."

Next, you should see a page to enter your name and email address you want associated with your profile.

Note: if you already have a LinkedIn® account and are

To join LinkedIn, sign up below...it's free!

First Name:

Last Name:

Email:

New Password:

6 or more characters

Join LinkedIn *

preparing to make some updates, do this first:

1. Go to "Settings" and look under "Profile" for *privacy controls* and look for *Turn on/off your activity broadcasts*
2. Click to remove the check mark and then save changes.

This will allow you to make changes without broadcasting each

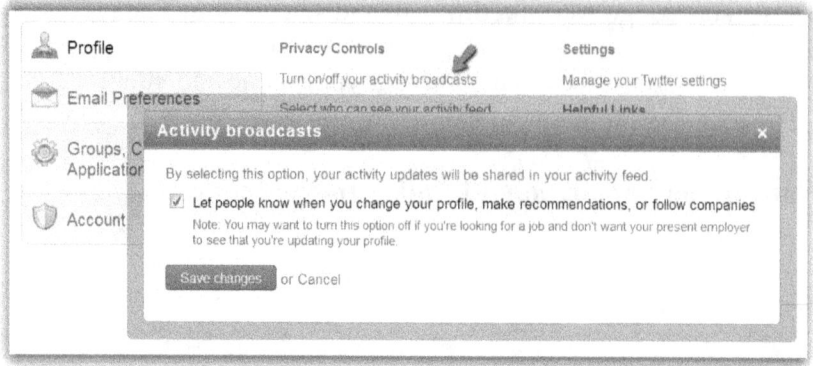

minor change to your network. When your profile is updated and refreshed, uncheck the box and broadcast away.

On the next page, you're required to input details related to your professional standing. Once this section is complete, LinkedIn® will offer to upload contacts in your address book. All contacts connected with an email can be imported to your account at this stage.

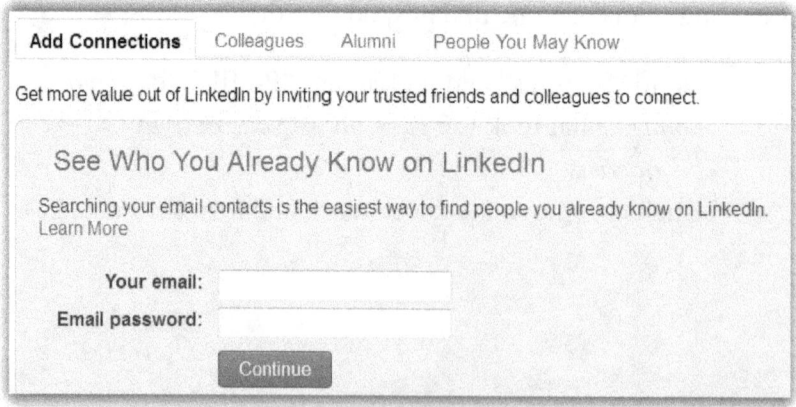

Getting the ball rolling to reach out to prospects on LinkedIn® couldn't be easier. But this is not the right time to send mass invitations. Choose "Skip This Step" at the bottom of the screen.

Next, LinkedIn® asks if you would like to manually enter email addresses to send invitations to colleagues.

Skip this step also.

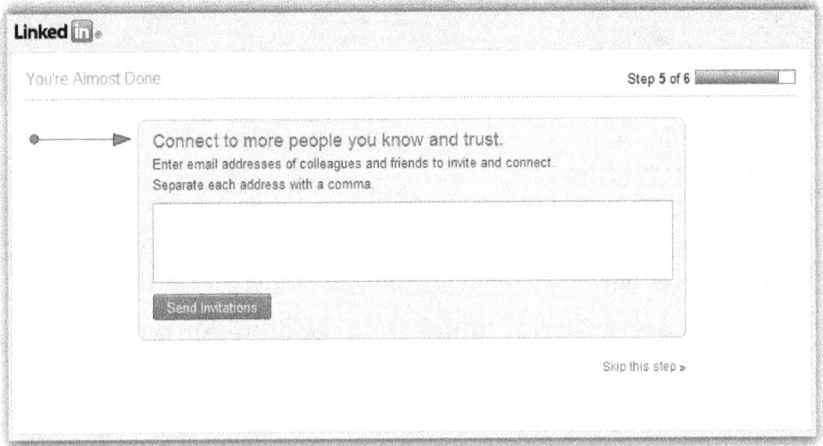

Selecting a membership plan is the final step for the first phase of completing your profile. As I mentioned before, the free membership will work for most people.

Completing Your Profile

Activating a basic account is only the beginning of establishing yourself on LinkedIn®. At this point, your profile is nowhere near finished. Essentially all you've created is a LinkedIn®

web page tied to your name and email address.

Bringing your profile up to speed requires more work, but is well worth the effort. The first place to start working is on your basic information. A well-written and complete profile is essential to maximizing your efforts.

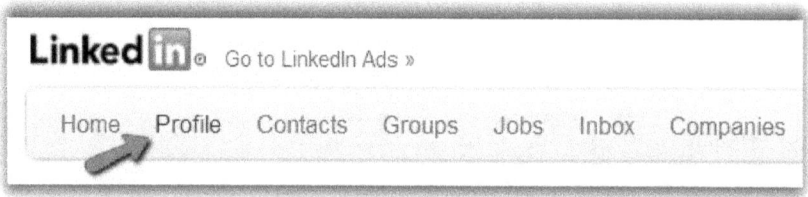

Edit your profile by:

1. Clicking the "Profile" menu from the Navigation toolbar.
2. Choose "Edit Profile" from the drop-down menu.

Profiles on LinkedIn® are formed in a résumé-style structure. In edit mode, individual entry fields are distinctly marked to enter specific information (i.e., summary and specialties) about you and your experience. Clicking the blue hyperlinks for each field redirects you to an entry form for that field. Guided prompts within the entry forms give ideas of what to add.

Your profile is a way for you to present yourself – as you want to be perceived. Your profile is available for review 24 hours a day anywhere in the world. No other personal branding communication tool has that kind of reach.

Your summary section should be a first person narrative, three to five sentences long. Begin sentences with phrases like:

- My background includes…
- Following graduation, I…
- While working in the xyz industry, I…

Try reading your summary aloud to hear how it sounds. Be aware of starting each sentence with "I" – which shows a lack of writing skills or self-awareness.

Write in your own voice. When in doubt, keep it short. Use key words, particularly in the summary and specialties sections – this is where LinkedIn' s search engine looks first.

Key word density is a buzzword I've been hearing about lately. It means that it is a good idea to repeat key words in the text to rank higher in searches. An example:

> Specialties:
> Commercial Real Estate
> Residential Real Estate
> Distressed & Foreclosed properties
> Real Estate training & education

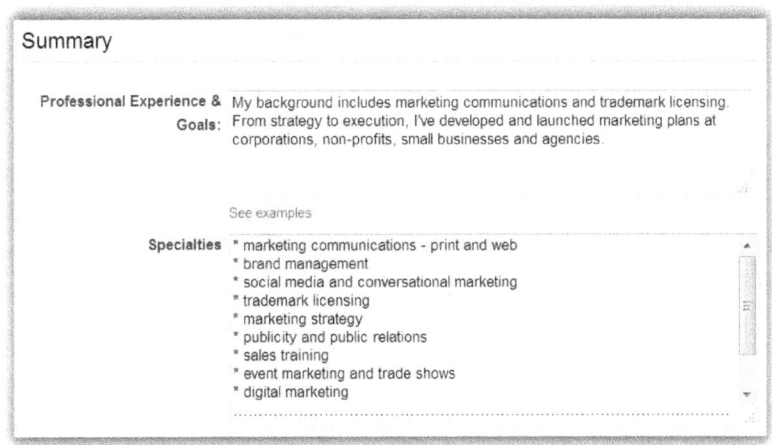

Summary

| Professional Experience & Goals: | My background includes marketing communications and trademark licensing. From strategy to execution, I've developed and launched marketing plans at corporations, non-profits, small businesses and agencies. |

See examples

| Specialties | * marketing communications - print and web
* brand management
* social media and conversational marketing
* trademark licensing
* marketing strategy
* publicity and public relations
* sales training
* event marketing and trade shows
* digital marketing |

Be especially diligent when you check your spelling.

 **Tip:** Write out your certifications <u>and</u> use the acronym. Example: PMP Certified, Project Management Professional.

Is it easy to misspell or mispronounce your name? Consider adding something like this:

My last name rhymes with "bagel" and is often misspelled "Nagle."

Anyone searching for you with the wrong spelling is more likely to find you. And now people know how to say your name. **Bonus points!**

Photos

Some people are reluctant to add a personal photo to their profile.

Concerns about being judged based on age or ethnicity are serious concerns. LinkedIn® gives search result priority to profiles that are 100% complete. In other words, incomplete profiles rank lower in searches. A profile is incomplete without a photo. We discussed some photo alternatives earlier.

Uploading a Picture

Be selective about the photo you use. LinkedIn® does not allow you to edit a picture once it's been attached. You can resize, but not edit, so choose wisely.

Lighting, distance, and facial composition are all elements to consider when making your choice. Business headshots are best for the professional environment at LinkedIn®. Lifestyle images, like what you'd expect at Facebook®, don't work well here. Especially, avoid pictures of you at your Cousin Pat's wedding, where you've cropped most of Pat's face out, but not all of it. C'mon, people, keep it professional.

Some folks have asked about attire and the answer is that it varies by industry. A suit in the entertainment industry might make you look stiff and unimaginative. Casual clothes on a CPA might make people nervous. What would you wear to meet a client or a vendor? That's probably a good choice for the photo shoot.

To attach your photo:

Select "Profile" from the navigation toolbar.

1. Click "Edit Profile" from the drop-down menu.
2. Once on the editing page, choose "Add Photo."

The next page allows you to upload an image. Browse your

Brandy Nagel Edit
Marketing Catalyst, author, social media coach, speaker
Greater Atlanta Area   Marketing and Advertising

directories to find the picture you want to post to your profile. Also, LinkedIn® provides a built-in photo-cropping feature to capture your headshot.

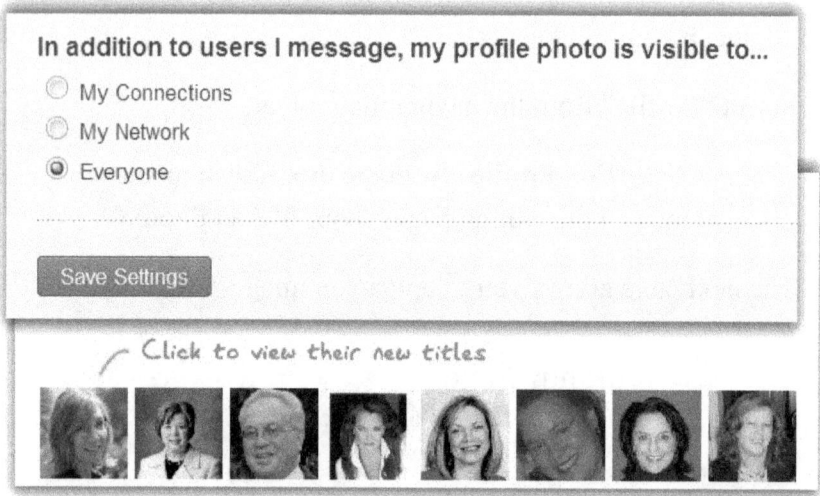

Current Photo

Upload a Photo
You can upload a JPG, GIF or PNG file (File size limit is 4 MB).

Browse...

Upload Photo or Cancel

After saving your photo, designate who should see your image.

In addition to users I message, my profile photo is visible to...
○ My Connections
○ My Network
◉ Everyone

Save Settings

Click to view their new titles

If you are still in some doubt about the importance of having a
good headshot, take a look at the e-mail I received from
LinkedIn:

Creating Your Headline

The headline area of a profile is prime real estate on
LinkedIn®. The information put into the headline segment is
important and should be strategically written.

Searching for people with LinkedIn's search function returns a
listing displaying only photos, names, and headlines. Knowing

this, you can understand why the content of your headline is so important.

To update your headline, from your profile's editing area, choose "Edit" next to your name.

The information you put in the "Professional Headline" field displays as the primary tagline at the top of your profile and in

---

Basic Information

Name

First Name:	Brandy
Last Name:	Nagel
Former/Maiden Name:	
Display Name:	◉ Brandy Nagel
	○ Brandy N.
	This option is disabled when you have a public profile. Change Public Profile Settings

Headline

Professional "Headline":	Marketing Catalyst, author,
	Examples: Experienced Transportation Executive; Web Designer and Information Architect; Visionary Entrepreneur and Investor. See more

---

LinkedIn® search results.

This is a great place to add your tagline or to use a catchy phrase.

Education and Experience

Next comes adding in your education and experience. No need to include all the details – but it is to your advantage to include specific accomplishments that highlight your capabilities.

As you add your work experience, avoid jargon that is only understood in that industry (or in that work place). Jargon does not explain value. So, I could say "I eliminated the need for TPS Reports." That probably meant a lot to my co-workers back then, but it's out of context for an outsider.

Here's the better way to express accomplishments:

- 800% increase in e-newsletter open rates in one year - from 200 to 1,600 readers.
- 90% reduction in annual printing costs, from $20,000 to $2,000.

These results are quantified for the reader, so she knows the value. How can you express the value you offer?

You must have some way to express how you…

> The difference between the almost right word & the right word is really a large matter--it's the difference between the lightning bug and the lightning.
> -Mark Twain

- Increased sales
- Increased profit
- Increased productivity
- Reduced costs
- Reduced waste
- Saved time
- Made a "headache" go away

As you fill in your profile, be specific. **Be bold**. Be accurate. This is no time to be modest.

Take your time and get the details right on your profile.

_____

_____

_____

Customizing Your LinkedIn® URL

By default, LinkedIn® assigns you a URL with random numbers and letters. For branding purposes, you will want to customize the link, even if you don't use it often. An easy-to-read website address increases the chance of people being able to remember and find you on LinkedIn®. Promote your LinkedIn® URL on your Twitter® and Facebook® pages, and email signature to drive traffic to your profile.

Customize your URL by:

1. Selecting the "Profile" menu from the navigation bar.
2. Click "Edit Profile" from the drop-down menu.
3. Scroll down the page until you see your "Public Profile" website link.
4. Choose the "Edit" function to the right of your link.

All LinkedIn® website addresses begin with www.linkedin.com/in/. On the next page, enter your preference for a unique URL to the LinkedIn® prefix. This could you your name, or a tagline. If your name is taken, try adding a slash between your first and last name, or add a middle initial.

Living a double life?

I've been asked, "What do I do with my two careers? Set up two profiles?"

Probably not – anyone looking for you by name will be confused to see two profiles. But it also depends upon what those two roles are. Insurance salesman by day, jazz guitarist by night? Use Facebook® for your music career. Mary Kay lady by day, oil painter by night? Try an online portfolio for your artistic endeavors.

8 More About LinkedIn®

LinkedIn® is a **gigantic database** that we, the users, maintain. We can count on LinkedIn® being accurate because we are individually responsible for maintaining our own profiles. Which is good. Your profile is not a static document, and it should change or evolve over time.

You are under no obligation to be 100% complete with your LinkedIn® profile. As a general rule of thumb, you should go back 10 years into your work history and/or your three most recent jobs. (This rule does not apply to your résumé, which must be complete and accurate.)

It is not necessary to share personal information on LinkedIn®, like your phone number, the county you live in, or birthdate.

Privacy Concerns

Many people are concerned about their privacy and identity theft. As an exercise, open up Google® and search for your name, in quotation marks, and the name of your street. Documents that have historically been part of the public record, such as property tax, are now available online, and some are searchable. It is entirely possible for someone to find out how much you paid for your house, and (sometimes) how much money you made last year. With this in mind, it is important to protect your privacy; you should not share information about your birthdate or hometown. We do not want to make it easy for identity thieves.

Also, remember to be vague about upcoming vacations. It is acceptable to announce you are excited to be heading to a dude ranch in Montana, but never include the dates. You can brag about your trip after you have returned. Please see www.pleaserobme.com for more information on this.

Public Profile vs. Private Profile

Certain segments of a profile can be restricted from public view by non-members. Whether you display all portions or restrict some, a public profile is an effective business tool. A public profile on LinkedIn® ensures your professional skills are presented to all people who desire to know more about you.

The next page in the set up process gives you the option to unselect areas for public view.

```
Customize Your Public Profile

Control how you appear when people search for you on Google,
Yahoo!, Bing, etc.

Profile Content
  ⦾  Make my public profile visible to no one
  ⦿  Make my public profile visible to everyone
       ☑  Basics
           Name, industry, location, number of recommendations
       ☑  Picture
       ☑  Headline
       ☑  Summary
             └ ☑  Specialties
       ☑  Current Positions
             └ ☐  Show details
       ☑  Past Positions
             └ ☐  Show details
       ☑  Publications
       ☑  Skills
```

Completing your profile

Regardless of how much of your profile is shown to the public,
it is critical to have a 100% complete profile. Incomplete
profiles rank lower in searches, so the manager who is looking
for a new vendor is likely to see the folks with completed
profiles (including profile pictures, complete histories and three
recommendations) first.

Your ranking is also improved by having a diverse and
extensive network of LinkedIn® connections. How many? In
my experience, having a minimum of 175 connections is

critical. People with fewer than 175 first-degree connections tend to not get as much traction. And **a diverse network is a strong network**.

Quality or Quantity?

How many connections do you have? How many connections do you need?

When I first started with LinkedIn®, I thought I would have a tight circle of people - people I trusted. People I would give a kidney to, essentially. Over time, my standards have evolved so that I am willing to connect with people that I have just met, or have met online, if I am comfortable saying "I would help this person advance their career." For me, that is the definition of a LinkedIn® connection: professionals helping each other with career advancement.

With that in mind, brainstorm who you should connect with. A few thought starters:

- Co-workers
- Classmates
- Neighbors
- Friends and Relatives
- Teammates
- Service providers
- Mentors/Mentees
- Customers and Vendors

Think of everywhere you worked, lived, volunteered, worshipped, hung out...you know hundreds of people.

_____

_____

_____

Importing Contacts

Now that your profile is finished, it's time to import contacts. Looking for people one by one could take a while. LinkedIn® provides several ways to streamline this process.

To import contacts:

1. Choose the "Contacts" menu from the navigation bar.
2. Select "Add connection" from the drop-down menu. There you'll find several choices for importing data.

Whether you decide to have LinkedIn® sync with an online email, manually enter contacts yourself, or import from a file, it is simple.

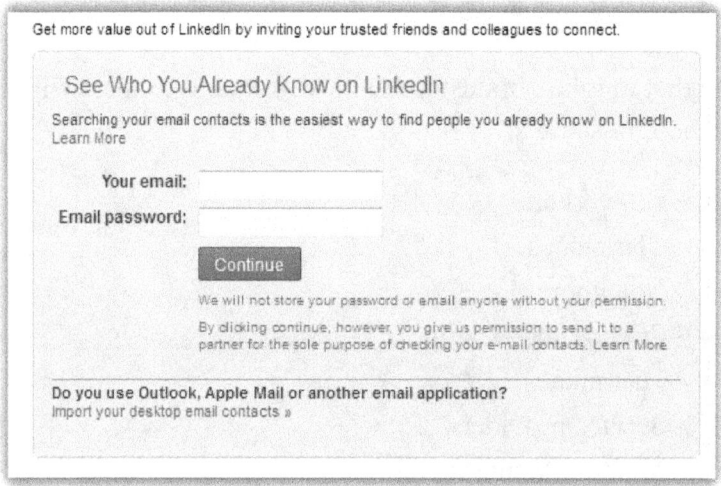

Also, you'll have the opportunity to approve and decline the additions of emails as LinkedIn® searches the designated online email box.

You can upload .csv, .txt, and .vcf files. Most desktop contact management applications, like Outlook, let you export addresses to one of the file types mentioned.

To use this feature, click on "Import your desktop email contacts." From there you can browse your computer files and attach the document.

Importing information does not automatically connect you with people. The next step is to send a personal invitation to each person. You can send the default message, but I've heard much grumbling about the default message. It has been likened to receiving a piece of junk mail addressed to "Occupant." It takes just a few minutes to write personalized invitations. Here are a few samples to get you started:

> *"Great to see your name on LinkedIn. I'm spending some time catching up with co-workers from XYZ Company – let me know if you have time for a quick chat."*

> *"Hey, I'm reconnecting with vendors I worked with at XYZ Company – and was happy to see your name pop up."*

> *"Good to see you are still with XYZ Company – let me know if you have time for a cup of coffee next week."*

If they accept the invitation, then you'll be connected. Adding the first round of contacts seems like a hassle. Keep in mind that all it takes are a few connections to gain access to professionals with the resources to help you land your next client.

LinkedIn® Groups

Joining a LinkedIn® Group introduces the opportunity to strengthen connections with like-minded individuals in an exclusive forum. The Groups function provides a private space to interact with LinkedIn® members that share common skills, experiences, industry affiliations, and goals.

You're allowed to ask to join any Group. For private groups, managers have the authority to accept or deny requests. The Group Directory lists all the groups currently on LinkedIn®. To search the Group Directory:

1. Select "Groups Directory" from "Groups" menu on the LinkedIn® navigation bar.
2. Click "Search Groups" box.
3. Enter a keyword or a group name in the search box. Narrow your search with the category and language selection. Click "Search."

Look for a group related to your industry. Join an alumni group – especially if you attended a prestigious school. The search results are typically ranked by size – largest groups to smaller groups. The larger groups give you visibility and access to more people, but the smaller groups often have more focused discussions and better opportunities to participate.

Join as many groups as you want – but do not show all of them on your public profile. Seeing 50 of these little logos makes your profile look like a Gremlin with a bunch of bumper stickers – not professional at all. Select the five to seven most important groups and make them visible on your public profile – the rest can remain hidden.

I started a group in 2009 to help me connect with local people in the Atlanta social media community. I made a simple logo and set up the **Atlanta Social Media Enthusiasts** group – it took less than 5 minutes. Currently the group has more than 500 members, many of whom are influential in the circles I move in.

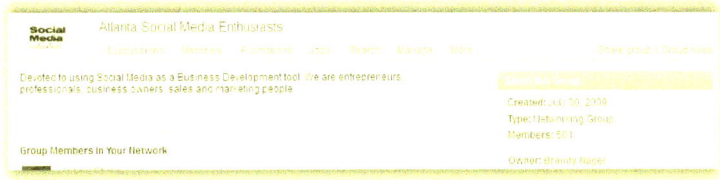

What kind of Group could you start?

_____

_____

_____

9 Advanced LinkedIn®

The Home Page – Your Personal LinkedIn® Headquarters

Status updates and announcements from your personal network are posted to the Network Activity portion on your Home Page.

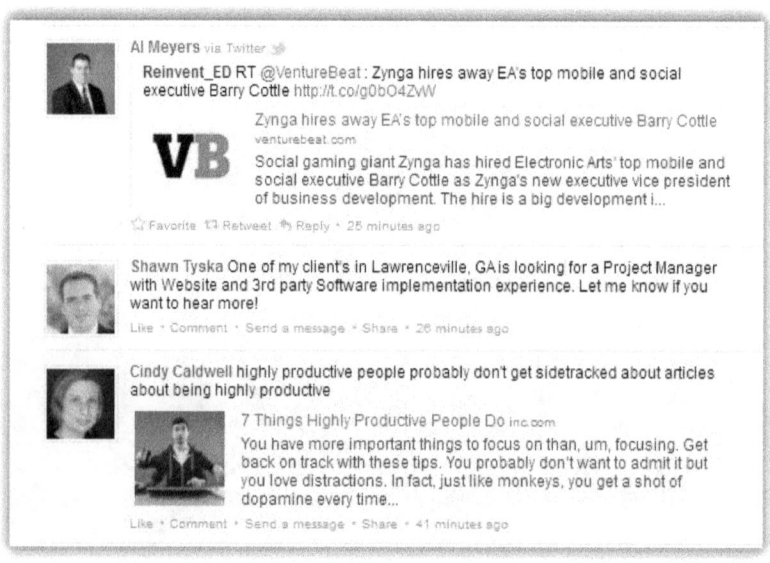

At a glance, the Network Activity area keeps you on top of what's going on with your connections. To make the most of your interactions on LinkedIn®, this is an area to check regularly.

Respond directly to individual updates without leaving the Network Activity area by clicking on "Like" or marking an update as a "Favorite."

Strategic Tip: Indicating that you like an update or leaving a comment could be discreet ways to gain the attention of people in your network who may be hard to connect with otherwise!

To broadcast your own updates, input messages into the empty conversation box and click "Share" to send messages to your entire network.

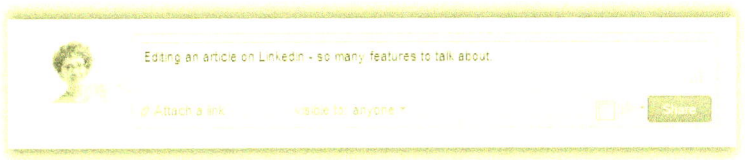

Sticky Situations

Disconnecting: Similar to de-friending on Facebook®, it is possible to disconnect from a connection. I have disconnected from one person because she was sending too many unsolicited e-mails promoting causes and events that were not relevant to me. When I disconnected from her, she was not notified, and I doubt she is even aware of the change.

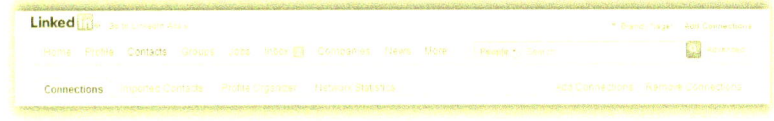

LinkedIn® Applications

LinkedIn® offers a handful of applications to enhance your profile. Applications act as automation tools eliminating the need to manually complete various tasks. Ideally, you want to spend more time networking instead of learning how to use applications. At the same time, it's best not to waste valuable energy clunking through busy work that can be minimized with the help of applications.

To add applications:

1. Click the "More" menu from the navigation toolbar.
2. Or select "Add an Application" from the lower right side of your Home page.
3. Or choose "Add an Application" from the sections area while editing your Profile page.

With the goal of highlighting your expertise on LinkedIn® in a streamlined manner, here are some recommended applications to get you started.

Tweets
by LinkedIn

Access the most important parts of the professional conversation with Tweets, a Twitter client you can use right on LinkedIn.

Tweets: Tweets connects your LinkedIn® Profile with your Twitter® stream. It's a Twitter® utility you can use directly from LinkedIn®. Quickly re-tweet and reply to tweets without ever having to leave the website. Personal updates and updates of people you're following show up on the sidebar of your profile.

Email Settings: Contact Settings and Receiving Messages,

Settings worth paying attention to are the Email Settings. Inmails and Introductions, found in the Contact Settings sub-category, fuel the ability for members to make connections through LinkedIn® beyond their personal networks. Later you'll learn more about Inmails and Introductions, and exactly how to use them. For now just know these features determine how accessible you are to the LinkedIn® community.

Furthermore, avoid missing important Inmails and Introductions by customizing how you're to be notified when you receive them. The Receiving Messages feature presents a detailed menu to specify exactly when and how often notifications are sent.

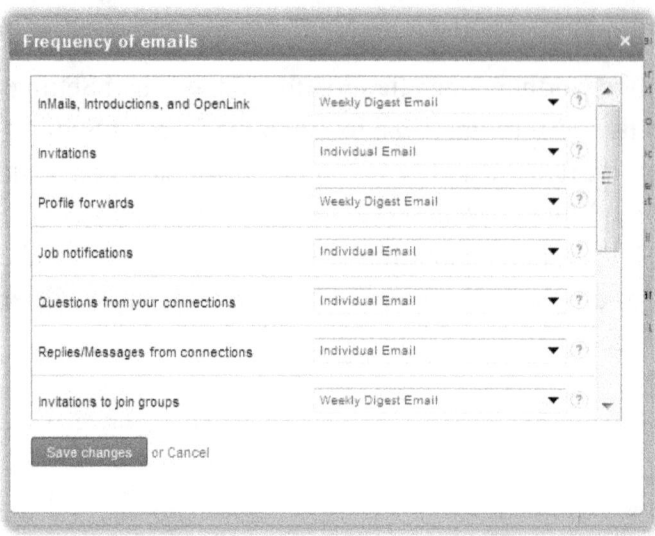

The Mechanics of LinkedIn®

After opening an account, creating a profile, and importing personal contacts, you're ready to move out into the larger network. LinkedIn® works for you based on who you already know. These folks are bridges to new connections.

LinkedIn® connections are on three levels. Your direct contacts are marked as 1st level, the contacts of your first level contacts are marked as 2nd level, and if someone is linked with a person who in turn is connected with one of your direct contacts, that person is tagged as a 3rd level contact. If you have no connection, then they're identified as "Out of Network."

Also, all of the contacts of your first level contacts are made visible to you. LinkedIn® even reveals the number of shared connections you have with a person, and the identity of the shared connections.

Introductions, InMails and Invites

As you come across profiles in the community, LinkedIn® displays several methods for adding the person to your network. Regardless if you're directly on a profile page or reviewing a listing of profiles from a search, generally these options are offered:

- Send InMail
- Get introduced through a connection
- Add to your network

On the profile page, you'll find this information in the upper right corner.

Introductions: Have We Met?

Facebook® has likes, Twitter® has re-tweets, and LinkedIn® has introductions. Designed around the principle of referrals, introductions are one of the best ways to meet new people on LinkedIn®.

The basic idea is that if you don't know a person who you would like to be connected to, find someone within your personal network who will introduce you to this person.

When asking for an introduction you are essentially writing two notes: a note to the Person You Want to Meet and a second note to the Middleman. Both parties will see both notes, so

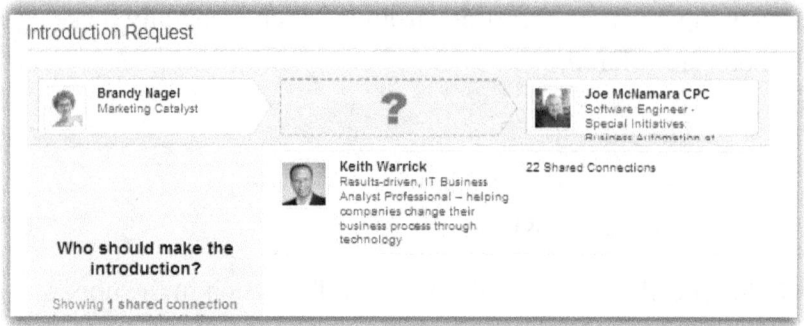

keep it professional and to the point.

My experience with these types of requests is about 50% success and 50% go nowhere. I've never had a bad experience (or bad advice) but I have had people ignore my request.

You've Got Inmails

On the other hand, InMails are a paid feature of LinkedIn® enabling you to send emails directly to a person's LinkedIn® mailbox, regardless if they're in your network or not. Depending on your account level, you'll receive a credit for a certain number of InMails per month. If you send an InMail but you don't get a response from the recipient after seven days, then your account is credited for the InMail.

Although InMails require payment and you're running a risk by contacting someone who doesn't know you personally, it's an effective tool for professionals to cut to the chase in developing targeted connections.

Inroads with Invites

Technically, you can send anyone an invite at any time. With the invite feature, you don't need a connection or a paid account to send one. However, it's advisable to use discretion with this tool. Recipients can respond by stating they don't know you, preventing you from sending the person an invitation ever again. If you receive too many "I don't know you" responses, LinkedIn® may restrict you from sending invitations altogether.

Building Credibility

Establishing yourself as an expert takes more than a polished profile. In the same way an offline networking group, like the Chamber of Commerce, expects more from its members than handing out brochures, so it is with LinkedIn®. In particular, LinkedIn® members want to see contributions specifically for the community.

Some strategic ways to demonstrate your expertise on LinkedIn® are with Recommendations and participating in LinkedIn Answers.

Recommendations

Similar to testimonials, connections can leave Recommendations on your profile. When you're just starting on LinkedIn®, it's a good idea to encourage people you've worked with to post their testimonials to your profile. A Recommendation stands as social proof from a third party that you're a skilled professional.

As stated by LinkedIn®:

> *Users with Recommendations in their profiles are three times more likely to receive relevant offers and inquiries through searches on LinkedIn®.*

If you choose to do so, recommendations will appear in two places on your profile page. At the top of a profile, LinkedIn® shows a Recommendation counter, while a detailed-view of each recommendation appears toward the bottom of a profile. Recommendations are visible to your personal network and Fortune 500 companies utilizing the LinkedIn® Recruiter Tool.

The simplest way to get Recommendations is to ask. To request a recommendation through LinkedIn®:

1. Select "Profile" from the navigation toolbar.
2. Choose "Recommendations" from the drop-down menu.
3. Click the tab marked "Request Recommendations."

And it is good karma to write recommendations, too. Who can you write a recommendation for?

_____

_____

10 YouTube®

Me? On YouTube®?

Heck, yeah! Make a series of videos using a webcam, Flip camera or a smartphone. It's easy, and it can be fun. Define the key terms of your industry or answer a burning question. Talk about best practices or how to avoid a common problem. Anything that sets you apart as a knowledgeable person in your field. Not ready to be a star? Create a curated channel.

Why You Want Your Videos on YouTube®

Primarily, it's free and it consistently works. YouTube® doesn't charge its users any money at all, unlike some other video hosting sites.

The only "cost" to using YouTube® is having AdSense ads show up along the bottom of your video, which most people simply close. (If you ever get to the point where you're getting millions of views on your videos, YouTube® will switch out AdSense for direct advertisers, at which point you'll be splitting revenues with YouTube®.)

Finally, YouTube® simply has more users than any other video platform on the planet. Twenty-four hours of video are uploaded every minute of every day. Over 2 billion videos are viewed on YouTube® daily.

People will see your video through the different category pages on YouTube®, from related videos and from your own site.

YouTube® has built a powerful platform designed specifically to get people to watch more than one video during each visit to the website.

Most people who land on YouTube® watch more than one video. This works in your favor, as people will jump from other videos to yours.

Components of an Effective YouTube® Video

The first thing you need to do when you're recording or creating a YouTube® video is to come up with a compelling topic.

The topic shouldn't be something that's already been done. If you're addressing a topic that's already been done, make sure that the video is either *much better* or *much more entertaining* than any other video out there on that topic.

Each topic should be either educational or entertaining; preferably both. The topic should somehow be related to whatever your website is about. If it's not, then find some way to tie it back to what your website is about. More on websites later.

To come up with topics for your videos, look at your industry and ask yourself:

- What are unsolved problems in my industry that I can address?
- What are common situations in my industry that I might address?
- What's a provocative way of thinking I can put across in my video?

Try to come up with videos that you think others would either find funny, intriguing, educational, or even thought provoking. It's much better to spark a discussion with a slightly controversial video than it is to create a boring video that's ignored entirely.

The key to choosing a great topic is to make it entertaining, *while* having it still be relevant in your industry. The videos don't have to be funny, they can also be educational. Whatever your style is, make sure your user gets something out of watching your video. If it's just commercial, the chances of the video "making it" are slim.

Video Content: Best Practices

There are a few rules of thumb you should follow for creating your videos.

First, shoot as much video as you can. Do multiple takes if possible. Then cut relentlessly.

You should have no more than two minutes of video when you're finished. Even if you shoot two hours of video, in the end most people's attention span simply doesn't go more than a few minutes. If possible go for several shorter videos rather than one longer video.

If your video is funny in nature, often times the best way to go is to simply use the best 30 seconds to two minutes in the video. Shorter videos tend to go viral more often than longer videos, because it's much easier to ask a friend to watch a one minute video than a 10-minute video.

Make sure the beginning of your video is attention catching. If the first 15 seconds of your video are boring, chances are you'll lose your viewers before they ever get to the best parts of your

video.

Keep your videos short, put an attention catching segment up front and make sure that all the content in the video is top notch.

Remember: Be liberal when shooting video, be ruthless when cutting video. Always let your video sit for a day or two and come back to it before publishing it. You'll see things with new eyes. Consider also showing it to a friend or two before launching your video.

Video Content: Calls to Action

The call to action is one of the most important parts of a YouTube® video.

The call to action is the part of the video when you tell someone to do something. For example, if you want them to click on a link and land on your LinkedIn® profile or blog, that's a call to action.

In the last few years, calls to action on YouTube® have really taken a leap forward. Today, you can create clickable annotations right in the video. You could create an attractive picture telling them to click on the picture, which then sends them to your website for more information.

To do this, use the edit video menu to add a clear annotation with a link. You can also use text box or speech bubble annotations.

Your *call to action* should be crystal clear about what you want your users to do. It should be towards the end of the video, rather than in the middle. People who put annotations in the middle of the video tend to annoy users rather than inspire action.

The call to action should link to your site, while still looking classy in the video. Consider these types of calls to action:

- Share (often with links to several sharing methods)
- Subscribe (more on this below)
- Email me
- Call me
- Visit my website
- Read my blog
- Check out my LinkedIn® profile

YouTube® has a policy of removing videos that were created solely for commercial intent; so make sure your video is really contributing something educational or entertaining, rather than just selling you.

Look professional – not spammy – with your calls to action. The call to action should last several seconds, added on to the end of your video. So, if someone watched your 2-minute video, at the end they'll see your call to action and see it for 10 seconds, for example.

Your call to action should also have a text version on the screen. Rather than just a clickable box, the screen should also have the URL. The reason for this is because there are still a lot of people who don't realize that you can click on annotations in a YouTube® video. You can help these people make their way to your site by having a link for them to go to as well.

Calls to Action: Subscribers

Rather than sending people to your website or to another video, one other common call to action is the subscribe call to action.

Subscribers will be notified whenever you post a new video. By getting more subscribers, you'll incrementally increase your viewership with every video you post.

Although a lot of people think that the video that goes viral is the way to go, often the people who are most successful on YouTube® are folks who build up a loyal following over time.

A subscriber call to action should be at the end of the video. Generally that takes the form of a speech bubble or call box directly under the subscribe button pointing towards the subscribe button.

Building your subscriber base is one of the major secrets to success on YouTube®. How is it that some people can post just about any video and get *millions* of people to instantly watch that video? It's their subscriber base.

You can have that kind of clout, too. Just create a compelling call to action in every video urging people to subscribe to your channel.

YouTube® Mistakes to Avoid: Copyright Material

Copyright infringement is a big deal. It can get your video removed if you're lucky, have your entire account shut down if you're unlucky, and could even result in a lawsuit if you're really unlucky.

To avoid copyright infringement issues, don't use copyrighted shows, movies, sounds or graphics in your videos.

There are plenty of websites with royalty-free sounds, pictures or videos. Some of these websites are free, while others require you to pay to use their content.

Even YouTube® provides you with a built in selection of **royalty-free music** that you can access in their video editor. With so many choices, there is simply no reason to use copyrighted material in your videos.

Some people think that their video can just slip past YouTube® and not get caught. The reality is that YouTube® has sophisticated filters that go through every video searching for copyrighted material. It's not reviewed by a person, at least at first, instead the audio and video in your uploads are analyzed by complex programs designed to spot and remove infringing videos.

Setting Up Your YouTube® Account Right the First Time

A small mistake made in the beginning of your YouTube® career can be devastating. Remember that once you start building a brand, it's hard to change it.

The most important decision you can make in this regard is your username. "level65druid" is not a good username unless you're creating gaming videos. Professional YouTube® accounts should have professional names.

If you already have a YouTube® account in a name that isn't great, just open a new account. It's so easy to create a new username; don't use a less-than-optimal name just out of convenience. There's nothing in YouTube' s policies against having multiple accounts.

Setting up more details in your profile can also really help. Although most people don't look at an uploader's profile, once someone becomes interested in you they'll want to learn more.

That's when they'll click on your profile to see what else they can find out about you. What they see should be a carefully crafted message.

For example, if you're an interior designer who's showing off his work, you could have amazing videos, but unless you let people know in your profile that you're for hire, you'll probably miss out on many potential clients.

Treat this as your résumé. It's your chance to put who you are and what you do in your own words.

Your personal description and your website URL are the two most essential parts of your profile. The description should tell people about your credentials and possibly include a mild call to action.

Submitting Your Videos

The process of submitting your video is both easy and not so easy. First, you need to select the keywords for your video. Then you need to write the description and choose your tags. Finally, you upload the video.

To get started, click the "Upload" button to access the upload page. Then you'll be presented with the box in which you can write your title.

Your title is *the most* important part of your video. If you have a great title, more people will click on your video. More people will link to your video. More people will pass it on to their friends.

A poor title will get a video ignored, even if the video itself is great.

The title for your video should fulfill several criteria:

- Include your main keywords.

- Convey the main story or concept of the video.

- Catch attention and get people to want to click on it.

Selecting **keywords** is a crucial part of the process. Start with using the Google® Keyword Tool to figure out what keywords get traffic in your industry or niche. Also do intuitive research by browsing message boards and other websites to figure out what other people care about in your market or industry.

Although not every video you upload needs to have keyword rich titles, at least a good portion of them should.

Once you have your title, then you need to write a great description.

The description serves several purposes: it tells people more about the video, it can answer additional questions that weren't in the video, it can tell people about you and it can link back to your website or LinkedIn® profile.

Finally, choose the best tags to go along with your video. Tags are much like keywords in that they help other people find your video. Brainstorm as many related tags as you can.

Once you're ready to upload, select the video file from your

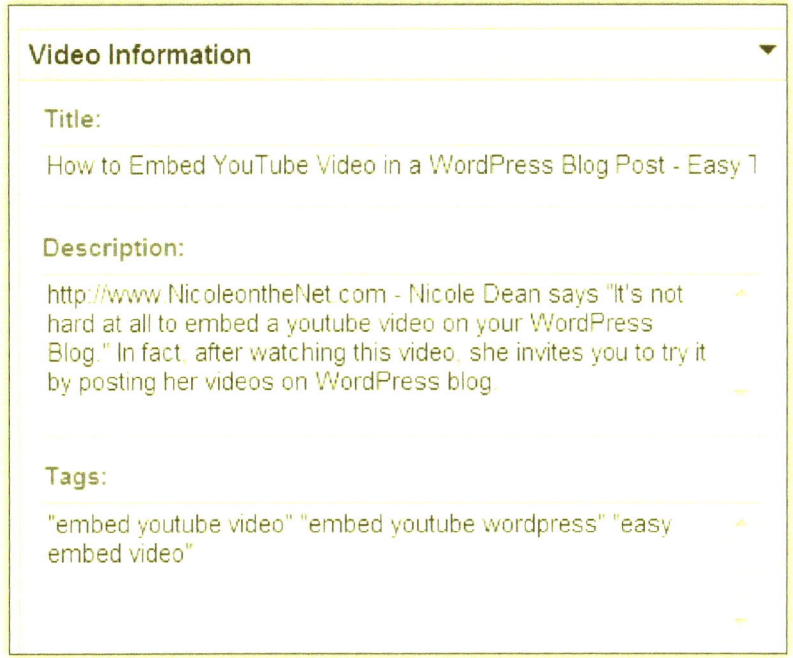

computer and press upload. As long as the video is in a format YouTube® understands (which includes avi files, mpeg files and mov files), your upload will begin immediately.

You'll see an upload bar with a percentage that shows you what percentage of your video is finished uploaded.

Embedding and Commenting

There are a few options you can choose on your YouTube® video.

The first option is whether or not you want to enable embedding. If you choose to enable it, that means anyone can embed the video on to their website. It means others can possibly pass off your content as your own.

That said, the benefits generally outweigh the risk. If the site with the embedded video gets a lot of traffic, that will result in increased view counts on your video, which increase the likelihood of more people seeing your video.

Since others embedding your video will generally not hurt you in any way, it's usually a good idea to enable embedding.

The other thing to consider is whether or not you should enable commenting. YouTube® is notorious for having a less-than-productive commenting community. If you enable commenting, you may get a few insulting or unintelligent comments.

Comments   ▼

 ⦿ Allow comments automatically

 ⦾ Allow friends' comments automatically, all others with approval only

 ⦾ Allow all comments with approval only

 ⦾ Don't allow comments

You'll also occasionally get intelligent comments that can help you build your credibility. Others will give you positive feedback. You'll also start to build something of a community online.

Finally, although YouTube® doesn't openly discuss their ranking algorithms, many experts believe that comments are part of YouTube's ranking formula. After all, if a video is getting a lot of comments, that means there's a lot of activity and that the video is relevant to the topic. Therefore YouTube® would rank it higher.

Whether or not you want to enable commenting is a personal choice. Decide what's best for you and your business.

Selecting a Video Thumbnail

Go to "My Videos & Playlists" to edit the video frame which shows for your video.

The video frame is the one frame people see when they're deciding if they're going to watch your video or not. That, the title and the view count are all people have to go on.

Naturally, the video frame has a large impact on whether or not people will make the split second decision to watch your video.

YouTube® doesn't allow you to choose your own video frame *unless* you're a YouTube® partner, meaning you have millions of views and are an advertising partner.

For most users, YouTube® will choose a random selection of frames from your video and pick one by default. You can instead choose which frame YouTube® displays.

Pick the frame that you believe will get the most attention. If none of the frames are good and you really want to change the frames, delete your video and re-upload it. YouTube® will again randomly take frames from different parts of the video, allowing you another range of choices for your thumbnail.

A Few Words on YouTube® Success

You now know just about everything you need to get started. Post your videos and consistently apply what you learned here.

In "Good to Great" by Jim Collins, a book that compiled results of interviews from hundreds of executives from top performing companies, Collins found what he called the "flywheel" effect.

Imagine you're pushing a giant, 50-foot-long metal flywheel. It might take you an hour to move it one foot. Then it might take you 45 minutes to move it the next foot. Then 30 minutes to move it the next.

Eventually the flywheel will pick up speed and move faster than you can push it, propelling itself forward with its weight.

Launching a YouTube® channel works similarly. The first few videos may not immediately hit, and it may feel like work. But if you keep putting the work in, eventually the momentum of your community will take off.

11 Facebook®

As the largest social media platform in the world, Facebook® is a good place to improve your visibility. Because Facebook® is a mutual opt-in relationship, you are visible only to people you have designated as friends and who have done the same to you. Staying on the minds of your friends can be an important part of a visibility campaign, so establish your presence, and visit Facebook® five times a week. Frequency of visits is crucial in the fast-paced world of Facebook®.

One way to connect with people on Facebook® is to contact them on their birthday. Update your account settings to receive an e-mail once a week with upcoming birthdays. Rather than send a generic birthday greeting, though, use the opportunity to send a real note with questions and an update.

> *"Hey Jodi, haven't talked with you for a while. Hope you and the kids are doing great. I haven't been to Seattle in months, but I remember how much you love it there. My real estate business continues to thrive. If you have any referrals for me, please send them my way. I'd appreciate your help. Give my regards to Tom."*

Keep it **simple** and be specific. The next step is to branch out from friends and try to connect with other people.

Facebook® Pages and Groups can effectively connect you to a group of people, but they tend to be social in nature, and less business-oriented. Consider the possibilities:

Create a Facebook® page for your professional association. This will put you in front of many new people. Here's how to create a Facebook® Page and Facebook® Group, as well as a few tips for success.

Step 1: Getting Started
Get started by going to http://www.Facebook®.com/pages/. Click on "Create Page."

Step 2: Choose Page Type
Select what kind of page you want to create.

Step 3: Name Your Page

93

Give your page a name. If Facebook® needs additional information, they'll ask for it here.

Step 4: Add Profile Image
Add an image from your computer. Pick an image that accurately represents your community. This might be the logo from your professional association, or a picture of the group together.

Step 5: Invite People
Once your page is up, it's time to get people to visit. There are two ways you can do this: By building friends, or by importing a contact list. The first option will send a Facebook® invite, while the second will take your existing contacts and let them know you've created a page.

Step 6: Edit Your Information
Click the "Edit Info" button at the top to edit your page details.

Edit your category and most importantly your description. You can also create a username for your page here.

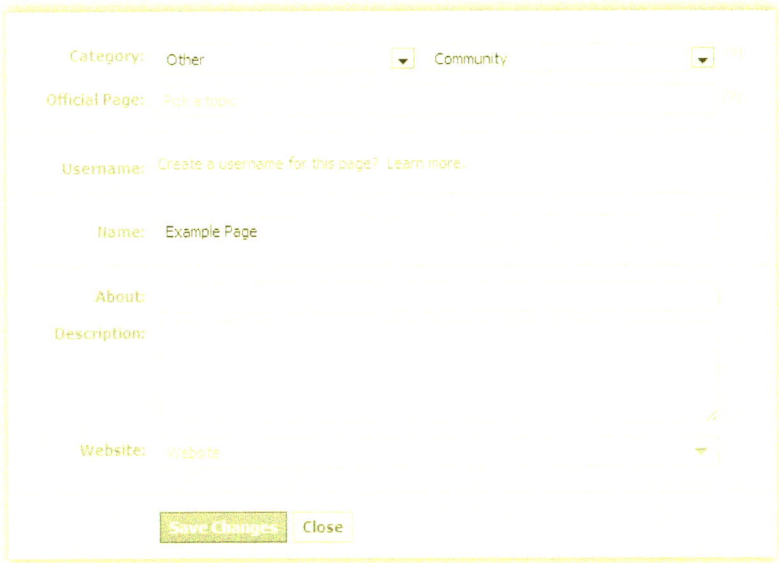

Step 7: Posting to the Wall

All that's left is to post content to your wall. Posting to your wall is like posting to any other wall on Facebook®. You can post text, as well as attach multimedia content and hyperlinks. One unique feature of pages is the ability to ask questions.

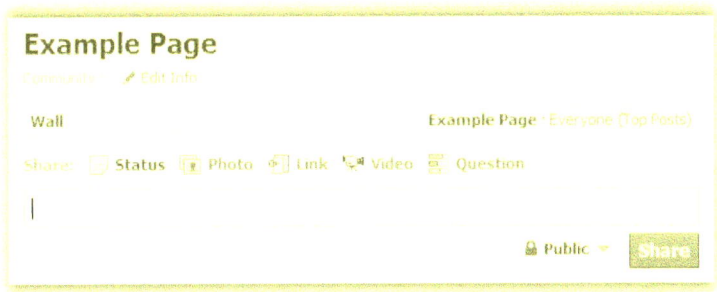

Alternatively, you could start a group for people with similar businesses interests – *Social Media Enthusiasts* or *Communication Professionals of Greenville*. While these are not hardcore industrial, they are professional in nature. And unlike a LinkedIn® group, these can be rather informal (and friendly – an opportunity to connect in a different way.)

You could create a group for your neighborhood ("*13th floor Residents of the Grand Oakes Building*") or homeowners association ("*Residents of Coleman and North Point Way*"). I didn't know where most of my neighbors worked until I connected with them through social media. Turns out, my neighbors are well connected.

Set up the page to start, and invite a few people that you think will participate and contribute. Online groups tend to be strongest when 1) one common element unites the group and 2) the group has some diversity. Groups can be Open, Closed, or Secret.

One of the groups I belong to has become a great place to pass along opportunities - speaking gigs, client requests – and a place to ask for referrals (does anyone have a recommendation for a great caterer?) Visit the group five times a week – post questions, link to articles, make comments. Create a presence for yourself by being present. Engage the other members with your consistent participation.

Tips for Running a Successful Facebook® Page or Group

1. **Short, Snappy Posts**. People on Facebook® will usually see your content through their feeds, or via email, rather than explicitly visiting the page or group. When you're appearing in their feeds, it's best to have short and snappy posts. This helps catch their attention and keep it. Overly long or boring posts tend to lose readership.

2. **Post Regularly**. Get people used to reading your content. Try to post on a regular schedule, daily if possible. Since a status update really shouldn't take more than 5 minutes to write, you can even write it all at once for the week and just post it at the end of the day every day.

3. **Have a Two-Way Dialogue**. Get your readership involved. Ask them questions. Have conversations. Don't just use your page or group as a one-way outlet of information and self-promotions. Instead, use it to talk with people.

4. **Respond**. If you don't respond regularly and quickly to comments and questions, people will simply stop engaging. On the other hand, if you respond quickly and regularly, people will enjoy participating more and do it more often.

5. **Use Multimedia**. Don't just use text. A few years ago, communicating through social media with just text was entertaining and engaging. Today however, to really catch someone's attention you should use a variety of media, including images and videos.

6. **Be Human**. Let them get to know you, who you are, what you stand for, and your personality. Don't be afraid to make a joke or let a little humanity come through.

12 Twitter®

Twitter® allows people to interact in a unique, spontaneous, and quick way. With Twitter®, you can post as often as you'd like. If you "spammed" Facebook® status updates or email messages, you'd be penalized. On Twitter® however, you could make a new post every hour and be commended for it.

Here's how to use Twitter® for visibility.

Step 1: Create a New Account

To create a new account, go to http://www.Twitter®.com. Fill out the new account form.

Step 2: Startup Wizard

Go through the startup wizard if it's your first time using Twitter®. Try to create a Twitter® handle that is short and descriptive.

You'll be invited to add people based on categories.

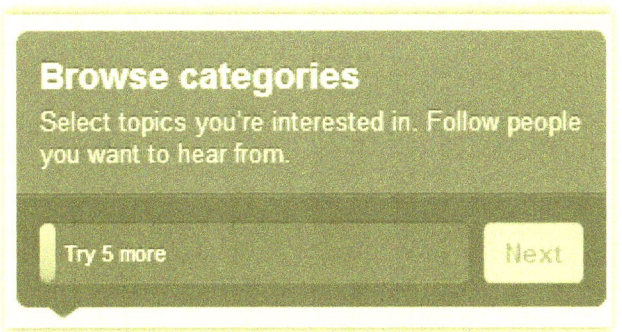

You'll also be invited to search for and add contacts based on your email address book.

Use the categories feature and the search contacts feature to set up your initial follow list.

Step 3: Posting New Tweets

To post a Tweet to anyone who's following you, type your message into the box on the left. Twitter® limits tweets to 140 characters. This will be sent out to all your followers.

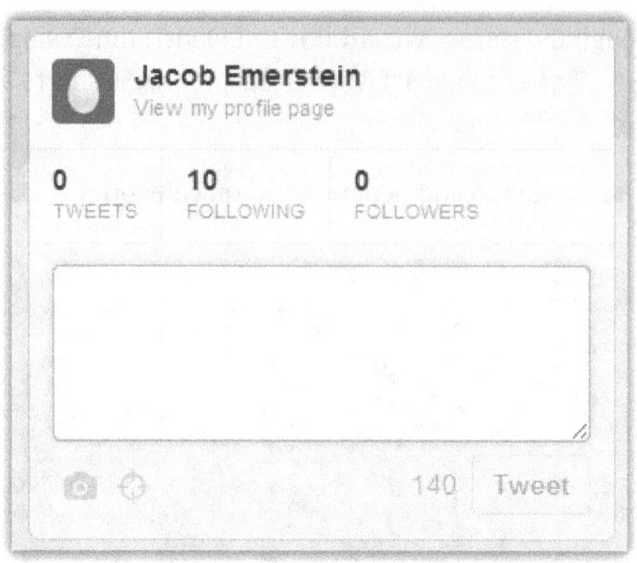

Step 4: See Who's Talking to You

When someone wants to talk to you or about you on Twitter®,
they use a *mention*. They do this by putting the @ symbol in
front of your name. For example, if your username was
Jacob123, they would tweet something and put @Jacob123 in
the tweet.

To see who's been talking about you with this feature, just go
to @ Connect along the top.

Note: If you and another tweeter are mutually following one another, you can communicate with direct messages. Otherwise, you have to use @ connects.

Step 5: Discover More People to Follow

To discover more people to follow, just click "Discover" along the top navigation bar. You can browse by category, by stories, by level of activity, by recommendations and by finding friends.

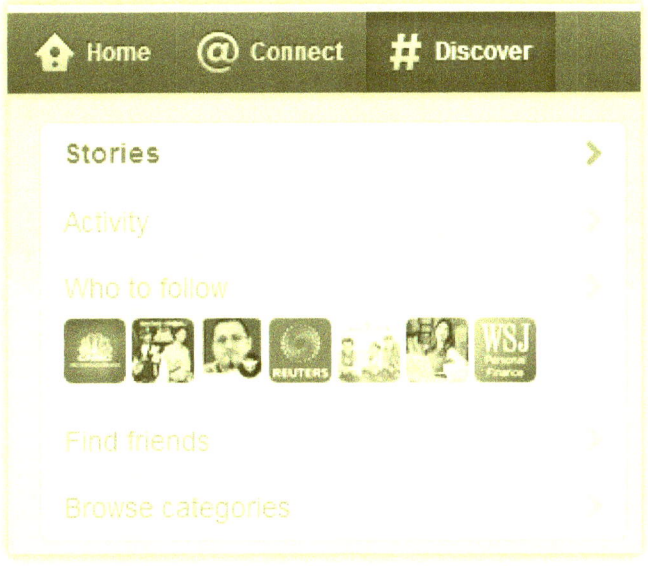

Step 6: Using the Feed

Once you've followed a handful of people, you'll be able to see their tweets in your feed. To reply, retweet or favorite a tweet, just hover your mouse over the tweet and click the corresponding button.

Here are a few tips for getting started, building your readership, and improving rapport.

1. Use outside tools. Twitter' s default interface is great for the casual user, but is missing many features for active users. For example, you can't schedule a tweet to be sent later. Use Twitter® applications, such as TweetDeck or HootSuite, that add functionality to Twitter®. Smart phone apps abound, too, for tweeting on the go.

2. Pay attention to your avatar and background. Having an avatar and background that resonates with your personal brand can work wonders. The moment someone lands on your Twitter® page, they should immediately feel like they're interacting with you.

3. Make it easy to follow you. Place a Twitter® link or button on your main website, in your signature block, on your blog posts, on your Facebook® pages and generally anywhere that people can find you.

4. Use RT *@name* to retweet. If you're retweeting something, make sure to use the "RT @name" format so you show up on their @ Connect tab.

5. Tweet regularly. The more often you tweet, the more your content will be seen by people. On Twitter®, it's very hard to tweet too often.

Twitter® is similar to a eavesdropping on a cocktail conversation – you can listen to several people, but are not required to respond to any of them. However, it is not enough to lurk on Twitter® – listening is important, but if your numbers look like this…

Following: 36   Followed by: 0   Tweets: 1

…everyone can see at a glance that you are not active on Twitter®.

The currency of Twitter® is immediacy and relevancy. So, tweeting about what you're eating is of no interest, but telling who you are having lunch with may be interesting – but only during lunchtime. I have never read a tweet that started "Last week I…" Twitter® lives in the now, yesterday is irrelevant.

The best way to get into the swing of Twitter® is to start re-tweeting. Then post a casual comment – stick to simple topics at first. Then post comments about industry news. Post an inspirational or witty quote from a book or article.

Tip: Always read the entire tweet – and click on the link to see what it leads to – before retweeting.

13 Google Plus

Google+ pages allow you to connect with Google+'s millions of users in a professional way. It helps you separate personal posts from business posts. Google+ also offers a number of unique features, such as the ability to segment who sees what on your page. Here's how to setup and use Google+.

Step 1: Getting Started
Start by going to http://www.google.com/+/business/.

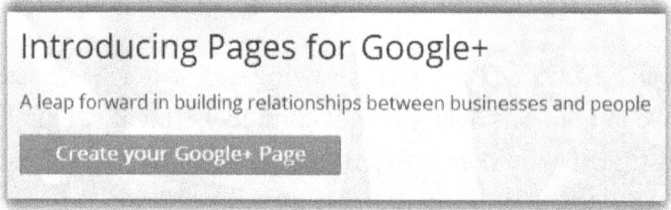

Step 2: Select a Category
Google+ has several kinds of pages you can create. Each has a different look and feel. Choose the one that best relates to the page you want to create.

Step 3: Basic Information

Fill out some basic information about your page. Set the name of your page, your website, and your privacy settings here.

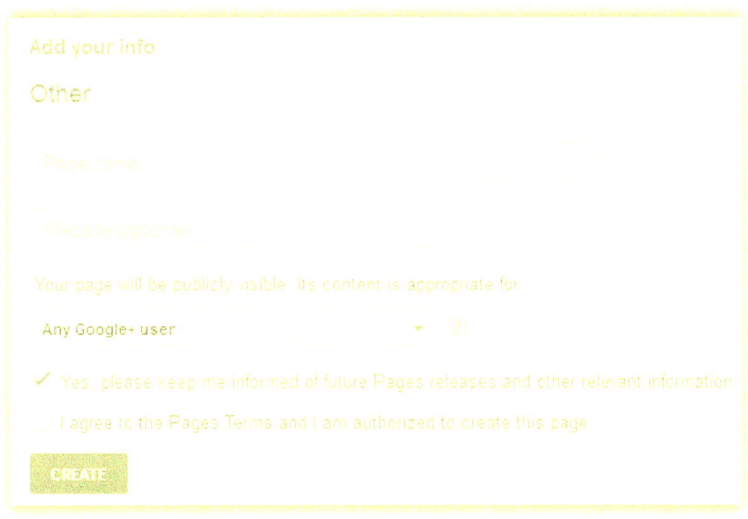

Step 4: Share Your Page

Once your page is up and running, Google+ will give you the opportunity to share it with the world. Just enter a brief message and it'll be posted to your wall.

Step 5: Posting on Your Page

Your page is now up and running. To begin adding content, just click "Post on Your Page."

There are a few important things to know about posting.

First, if you want to post an image, a video, or a web link, just click the corresponding button on the lower right corner. Any photos or videos you post will be added to the "Photos" or "Videos" tabs.

You can customize whether you want the post to be visible to everyone, or just a select group of people by canceling "Public" in the lower left and adding specific circles that you want to post to.

Google+ pages offers a few unique features that no other social networks offer. Taking advantage of these features will help you gain more followers and build more credibility and visibility.
Here are a few tips for using Google+ pages.

1. Use your circles. Separate the different interest groups in your user base and post different messages to them.

2. Take advantage of the multimedia options. Google+ allows you to embed images and videos inside the post itself. All the multimedia you post can be easily accessed in the Photos or Videos tabs.

3. Post long pieces of content when it makes sense. Unlike other social networks, which cut off your content and require you to link, Google+ pages allows you to post it all on your wall.

4. Actively promote your page to your Google+ friends and circles. While Google+ pages can be a powerful tool for communicating, people simply won't hear about it unless you talk about it often.

5. Assume your audience is sophisticated and tech savvy. The majority of Google+ users are early adopters and people who like to test new technologies. As a result,

by and large your followers will be very savvy. Don't give out basic content; instead use your Google+ page to promote only the best of what you have.

Things you should *never* post on social media sites.

- Detailed contact information
- Personal travel plans
- Usernames and passwords
- Mother's maiden name, name of your first pet and other common password hints

14 Blogging, Podcasts & More

In addition to the Fab Four of social media, many other sites can contribute to your visibility campaign. Forums that focus on your industry, niche blogs by thought leaders, and Meetup boards have possibilities. Look for places where you can *contribute to* or *curate* the conversation.

Great places to answer questions and present your knowledge include Quora (http://www.quora.com/) and LinkedIn®, as previously discussed.

It is not always necessary to create new content. Curating existing content – that is, helping readers making sense of what is already out there – is a worthy strategy, also. This could be in the form of an e-mail newsletter or e-magazine.

Note: MailChimp.com offers a great free e-mail newsletter service. Also look at

- MySyndicaat – http://mysyndicaat.com/home
- Scoop.it – http://www.scoop.it/
- Storify – http://storify.com/
- Curation Station – http://curationstation.com/

You can start your own conversation on a blog or a Tumblr. A blog requires writing a post every week – or more frequently if possible. Tumblr is a visual micro-blog, especially valuable to anyone in the visual arts.

Tip: Visual creatives should look at Pinterest.com, too, to create a virtual pin board.

What will you blog about? The best blogs are either

1) focused on one topic and never stray or
2) a happy mix of current events, industry/business news, and personal notes.

Getting the proportions right on a mixed blog is an art, not a science. But know that future clients are interested in the quality of your thinking, not than the details of your home life. And revealing too much about your home life can work against you.

Before you invest in the setup of a blog, do yourself a favor and write your first ten posts. If you can't write ten, take it as a sign that you are not meant to be a blogger. There are so many abandoned blogs out there – make sure yours is not one of them.

Once you have your ideas for a blog, it is a simple step to use the same content to create a podcast, a slide show, or a series of articles for a website. In addition to my podcast, I write profiles on local entrepreneurs and submit the article to Patch.com. Slideshows (often created using PowerPoint) can be shared via SlideShare.com.

Top 10 Traffic Ideas for your Blog

Blogs are a popular way to create an online presence. You can build a blog for free and begin posting content right away. But, what good is that content if no one is reading it?

Of all the successful blogs on the Internet, hundreds more have failed. Unless you are willing to put the time in and treat it seriously, you won't be blogging long.

That is not to say that the failed bloggers weren't serious about blogging. Mostly, new bloggers aren't prepared for the work that goes into creating a successful blog. Just building the blog doesn't mean that people will necessary come to you.

Here are ten ideas to bring in the traffic your blog needs to survive.

1. Fresh Content – no one wants to visit a blog day after day and see the same posts. Update your blog content at least twice a week. This will be easier if you write several posts ahead of time and schedule them to publish in the future.

2. Article Marketing – the niche you've chosen for your blog is one that interests you. If it is interesting you will spend more time doing it. Create content not only for your blog but also to be submitted to article directories. Use the resource box to advertise your blog so people can find you.

3. Social Networking –. Join Facebook®, Squidoo, Twitter®, or a dozen others and make connections.

4. Viral Marketing – this is where you spread the word about your blog. Talk to friends, family, and even strangers. Give out business cards that have your blog address on them.

5. Use RSS Feeds – RSS stands for "Really Simple Syndication." Readers can subscribe to your feed and get email updates when new content is posted. It is an easy way for them to keep up with your blog.

6. Submit Blog to Search Engines – doing this allows your blog to be ranked. Google® and Yahoo! are two of the most popular search engines you want to crawl your blog pages.

7. Joining Forums – as a blogger you are a budding entrepreneur. Right now, you are marketing yourself to find traffic. Become a member of business forums, and others to meet new people and share ideas. Add a link to your blog in your signature line so others can find you.

8. Visit other blogs – show your appreciation to those who visit you by also posting comments on their blogs. It is a kindness that shows others you are part of the community. Add links to your blog in your comments.

9. SEO Marketing – whatever you write, use relevant keywords. Base your keywords on research you do to find the most popular words used in search engines for your niche.

10. Social Bookmarking – submitting posts to social bookmarking sites allows others who are members of those sites to track you back to your blog.

Using any of these ideas will start the traffic moving in your direction. It takes time but you will build the readership you want.

15 It's all About Attitude

You need to put the best possible light on everything.

I shovel elephant poop at the circus = I'm in show business, backstage operations.

> Worry about being better; bigger will take care of itself.
>
> — Gary Comer, American entrepreneur, founder of Lands' End

This is not lying, nor even exaggerating. It is simply perspective. And having that perspective is all about attitude.

Yo, create a common vocabulary with your peeps

(see what I just did there?)

A great source for all of the latest slang is www.urbandictionary.com.

Using slang can be fun…and it can make you look silly.

Rules for using slang:

- Be absolutely, positively sure you know what it means.
- Ease into it. Add one or two words to your repertoire at a time.
- If anyone rolls their eyes at you, stop immediately.

A friend of mine was using slang without knowing exactly what it meant. Unwittingly, she used a slang term with a sexual connotation to refer to a high-powered sports car. Boy was her face red. Remember people, urbandictionary.com is your friend.

Fine print: be cautious with words that have a sexual innuendo. I will not be held responsible for slaps or lawsuits. There, you've been warned.

Sometimes you have to make up a word, like "destuckify" – Havi is the master at this. (What does it mean? Google® Havi and you'll find out.)

Attitude and More

Have you met a man or woman who has given up on looking good? I have, and it is disappointing, and a little sad. Make the most of what you have – and don't fight it.

We have tons of commercial messages bombarding us every day – telling us we are too tall, too short, too fat, too thin, too grey, not blonde enough….whatever. You don't have to be perfect. And you don't have to conform to anyone else's standards.

Some say perfection is unattainable. According to the Japanese concept of wabi-sabi, perfection is less interesting.

Corporate trainer, Paula Leonard once told me, "Perfection has no personality."

I say, nothing you do has to be perfect – it just has to be fabulous.

Wabi-sabi is a Japanese concept or aesthetic, sometimes described as one of beauty that is "imperfect, impermanent, and incomplete"

Leonard Koren, *Wabi-Sabi: for Artists, Designers, Poets and Philosophers*

Looking the part:

Every time you leave the house, you have a chance to make an impression on someone who can help you land your next client. Hire a stylist if you need to. At the very least, make an effort to be well groomed every time you walk out the door.

Atlanta-based Certified Image Professional Karen Hughes offers these suggestions:

It's the little things that add up to a lot in developing your reputation and selling yourself. Maintain a positive image, follow these easy, effortless tips and you will be well on your way to creating a reputation that communicates success every time!

Ways to Show Up for Success

1. Keep your **shoes polished and current**. Men: a well-polished leather lace-up shoe will transcend the decades. Belts and shoes should match. Ladies: make sure that your shoes are not scuffed or worn at the heels. 2-3 inch heels are appropriate (if you can't walk comfortably, wear shorter heels.)

2. You clothing must **FIT** your body. No bulging tummy, no pulling, or gaping holes from fabric being too tight. Fit the largest part of your body and then alter to fit the rest of your body. Poorly fit clothing conveys a lack of confidence even if you have confidence.

3. Carry a **nice pen**. Yes, a nice pen will make you stand out. Do not carry anything plastic.

4. **No over-sized watches**. That means no trendy "toy" watches, or sport watches. If you don't have a watch with a simple face and leather band, don't wear one.

5. Carry a **portfolio** (leather) that will contain your résumé or networking profile.

6. Know how to **deliver a good handshake**. Aside from your first impression, a good handshake will tell people that you are confident and ready to engage.

7. Hair should be **clean and well groomed**. Clothes should be clean and pressed. Men: be clean-shaven. (People look to your facial expression and facial hair can hide this). Women: if you have long hair (below shoulders) tie it back to the nape of your neck or pull it up.

8. Men: no earrings, one watch, and one ring if you wear a ring. Women: **minimal jewelry**, no multiple piercings, or bracelets.

9. Always think in terms of 3 pieces (jacket being your third piece). Women: skirts worn to knees and with hosiery. Men: two-piece matched suit is appropriate. Socks should be to the knee (don't want to see your legs.)

For more from Karen Hughes, visit http://www.styleyouniversity.com.

Make Stuff Up

Well, good stuff, not just random stuff. Remember to use your power for good, not for evil.

In some industries, the rules are clearly defined and there are no grey areas. In other parts of the business world, grey dominates.

But most people want guidelines - even if they don't always follow them. So sometimes you have to make up a rule when 1) there is a need and 2) there is no existing rule.

Example: Having a picture on your LinkedIn® profile makes your profile more effective – and will improve your find-ability. When I ask people why they don't have a picture on their profile the response was often for reasons related to vanity: weight gain, grey hair, etc.

So, you may remember, I made up a rule. You have to have a picture on your profile, but it does not have to be a recent photo. My rule is 10% of your age.

> Never look for permission from someone else, but find a way to give yourself permission to do whatever it is you want to do more than anything else. Then when you find that, go for it full-tilt in spite of the fear and insecurity that we all have.
>
> -- Chris Guillebeau

This rule is completely arbitrary. I did not consult with anyone. I made it up. And it seems to meet a need for people who are struggling with this issue of which photo to use.

Amazing Grace

As your visibility campaign progresses, you may find yourself in awkward situations. Someone may ask your opinion in a setting where you don't want to share. Someone may ask for advice that you don't want to deliver at the spur of the moment. Or someone may ask you a question that is outside of your field of experience.

When you don't know what to say – or don't want to say what's on your mind, ask a question.

And a few words about **confidence**. Be who you are. Be the best at it.

Let your curly hair be curly or your straight hair be straight. Quit fighting your DNA and learn how to maximize it.

Finally, let's review the differences between arrogance and confidence.

Arrogance…	Confidence…
Interrupts	Listens
Says, "if you don't agree with me you are wrong."	Says, "tell me more about why you think that."
Insults	Inspires
Laughs at others	Laughs with other people

Who would you rather spend time with?

There are only three things any of us have any real control over and those are attitude, what we think about, and how we spend our time. Control those instead of trying to control the outcome of the situation you find yourself in and the possibility of good results are greatly increased.
– Mariette Edwards, The Executive Coach for High Achieving Creatives, Mavericks and Key Players Up To Big Things, www.doyourgreatwork.com

16 The Wrap Up

How to pull this all together?

Create an **online hub** –your LinkedIn® profile or your website or blog. Set up all of your other sites (Twitter®, Facebook®, etc.) to point to your hub. Keep it updated and fresh, it is your primary residence online.

A communication calendar (sometimes called a digital plan) will make it easy to keep track of your commitments – a weekly blog post, Twitter® chats, curating for Google+ and so on.

Participate in local activities in your community. Get your face out there. When you meet new people, exchange business cards and ask if you can connect on LinkedIn®.

If you discover a lack of local events that bring you in contact with the people you need to meet, **create an event**.

Hang out at the same place (coffee house or co-working facility) so the barista gets to know you. This creates a stomping ground – a place where everybody knows your name. Your comfort level will increase and that **confidence** will show when you meet new people.

And for the 20% of the population who are not terrified of **public speaking**, getting in front of a crowd is a fast and powerful way to develop your reputation. Provide a free class at local recreation center, offer seminars through the local library, or serve as a panelist at your professional association's next lunch and learn.

Use all of the online and off-line tools at your disposal to make a name for yourself.

Now go forth and **get famous**!

<u>Additional Resources</u>

Recommended Reading

How to Get Your Point Across in 30 Seconds or Less by Milo O. Frank

The Art of Possibility: Transforming Professional and Personal Life by Rosamund Stone Zander and Benjamin Zander

The Elements of Style by William Strunk, E. B. White and Roger Angell

In Style: Style 101 by Editors of *In Style Magazine*

Relevant Websites

http://about.me/

http://curationstation.com/

http://en.gravatar.com/

http://faceyourmanga.com/

http://mailchimp.com/

http://makeup.pho.to/

http://mysyndicaat.com/home

http://namechk.com/

http://personas.media.mit.edu

http://pinterest.com/

http://pipl.com/

http://plancast.com

http://pleaserobme.com/

http://storify.com/

http://www.behance.com/

http://www.brandynagel.com/

http://www.clippings.me/

http://www.eventbrite.com/

http://www.everystockphoto.com/

http://www.executivebomb.com/

http://www.Facebook.com

http://www.google.com/+/business/

http://www.google.com/alerts

http://www.onlineidcalculator.com

http://www.linkedin.com/

http://www.meetup.com/

http://www.micromentor.org/

http://www.patch.com/

http://www.quora.com/

http://www.scoop.it/

http://www.slideshare.net/

http://www.spokeo.com/

http://www.toastmasters.org/

http://www.tumblr.com/

http://www.Twitter.com.

http://www.urbandictionary.com/

http://www.vistaprint.com

http://www.visualcv.com/

http://www.volunteermatch.org/

Networking Profile: Fill in the Blanks

NAME

email@email.com   phone number

Executive Profile

[one or two sentences here to summarize your skills, abilities, education, and experience. Emphasize the goods or services you offer.]

Professional Experience

[Most recent gig – most recent title]

[Previous gig – previous title]

Target Client

[Define your perfect client right here.]

Education/Certifications (if relevant to your work)

[Highest level of education received, name of institution, city and state]

Community Leadership

[list meaningful volunteer activities]

127

Checklist: Setting up a LinkedIn® Account

This checklist covers the steps necessary to create and setup a LinkedIn® account.

☐ visit LinkedIn' s home page and click on "Join Today" to open a new account.

☐ enter your name, email address, and a unique password, and then click on "Join LinkedIn®" to continue.

☐ add professional profile details, including employment status, country, zip code, company name and job title, then click on the blue "Create my profile" button.

☐ search for contacts you want to connect with, clicking on the "Find Contacts" button as necessary to choose contacts to add.

☐ send personalized invitations to friends you want to connect with on LinkedIn®.

☐ Additional Profile Information.

add attachments for any résumés, letters of recommendation, or other information.

add both past and current Employment information, Education details, Websites, and a Twitter® account.

upload a profile picture Choose a photo that best represents you, and puts forth the professional image you want to convey.

□ create a profile headline that accurately reflects your experience and includes appropriate keywords related to your niche. This is an important step, since this is the primary tagline that appears next to your name when someone searches for you on the site.

□ choose between a Public and Private profile, by clicking on the "Edit" link next to the line for Public Profile. You can set options for various parts of your profile to be available for public viewing or not.

□ join any LinkedIn® groups related to your profession, niche, or industry, or create a group of your own. You can access these options by clicking on "Groups" from your main profile page.

LinkedIn® is one of the more useful social networks online, since it stores details about your profession, your industry, and contact details that help people connect with you through the site's network.

Top 5 LinkedIn® Tips for Creative Talent

Think LinkedIn® is for sales weasels and three-piece suits? Think again! Professionals from all industries use LinkedIn® to network, find opportunities, and engage in conversations.

How can you make LinkedIn® work to your advantage? Follow these simple tips:

1. Give it 100%

Complete your profile with a professional photo, and career highlights. Keep it concise - most people will scan your profile – not read it.

2. Get Recommended

Recommendations can help you stand out among a crowd of candidates. The easiest way to be recommended is to **give** recommendations. Take 10 minutes every week to write a few meaningful words for former co-workers, business partners or vendors. LinkedIn® asks them if they'd like to return the favor!

3. Get Connected

Connect with people you know and trust. Think about people you know from work, from school - even from the old neighborhood. Personalize your invitation and take the opportunity to reconnect with folks you have not talked with in a while.

4. Add your Portfolio to your Profile

Use one of the add-on applications to show off your skills: Behance (http://www.behance.net/groups/linkedin) or SlideShare (http://www.slideshare.net/) are great ways to showcase visual design skills. Copywriters can use one of the blogging apps (WordPress) to show a variety of writing samples.

5. Be a Joiner

You can join up to 50 LinkedIn® Groups. Look for groups related to where you are in your career - and where you want to be next. Joining a group gives you more visibility – and allows you to access people outside of your network. Select which group logos you want to display on your profile page - showing too many logos can make your page look cluttered and chaotic.

Quick Tips to Get Blog Traffic Fast!

Online, one of the keys to success is getting website traffic. The more visitors you have, the better your visibility. Here are five quick and easy tips to get website traffic fast!

Tip #1 Make sure you're tagging your keywords.

Do you spend a lot of time optimizing your content and then neglect to tag them on your webpage? Tags are where search engines look and if there are no tags, they'll pass right by your web pages. Here's a quick brief on tags.

Tip #2 Add content to your site daily.

Content is essential for traffic and a top search engine ranking. Content is what search engine spiders look for and index - without it there's nothing to index or rank. Give visitors and search engines a reason to visit and index your site. Make a commitment to provide daily, optimized content and your traffic will soar.

Tip #3 Cultivate valuable and relevant incoming links.

The more websites which link to your webpages the more valuable search engines perceive you to be, though not all links are created equal. Search engines give more leverage to links from sites which are popular and credible and from sites which are relevant to your website topic.

There are different types of links.

- A direct link looks like a basic website address, for example, www.yourwebsite.com
- A text link occurs when the webpage address is embedded in the text. Readers simply click on the link and are redirected to a new website page.
- If the link is to an internal web page, for example, an

article published on a website, rather than the home page, it is called a "deep link."

You can encourage linking to your website by:

- Adding content to your site.
- Submitting to article directories.
- Publishing press releases.
- Blogging and participating in social networking forums, chat rooms and social networking sites.

Tip #4 Be Social!

Now more than ever before, building a business is about building a community. Sites like Facebook® and Twitter® can be powerful tools for generating links and traffic to your site – create a profile and then post comments, links to your site and ideas to generate conversation.

Get involved - many chat rooms and forums are industry specific, so find those which cater to your industry and begin participating. Speak to and connect with a highly targeted audience.

Brandy Nagel

Brandy Nagel is an entrepreneurship educator at Georgia Institute of Technology. She works with students and faculty to build startups. She currently spends time every year in Puerto Rico, cheering on the incredible entrepreneurship ecosystem developing on the island.

Before joining Georgia Tech, Brandy traveled the Southeast coaching executives on how to use social media for business and career development.

Brandy has spent more than a decade in marketing agencies and in the private sector. She coaches business owners and executives on using social media. A frequent speaker, Brandy regularly presents on entrepreneurship, social media and personal branding. She received her B.A. in business from Brenau University and earned her MBA at Mercer University.

www.DigitallyFamousTheBook.com

www.ingramcontent.com/pod-product-compliance
Lightning Source LLC
Chambersburg PA
CBHW051215170526
45166CB00005B/1911